The Babysitter's Survival Guide

Fun Games, Cool Crafts, and How to Be the Best Babysitter in Town

BY **JILL D. CHASSÉ, PhD**

ILLUSTRATED BY
JESSICA SECHERET

The Babysitter's Survival Guide

Fun Games, Cool Crafts, and How to Be the Best Babysitter in Town

BY **JILL D. CHASSÉ, PhD**

ILLUSTRATED BY
JESSICA SECHERET

STERLING

New York / London
www.sterlingpublishing.com/kids

Dedicated to the two who teach me
oodles about child development on a daily basis,
my son Malachi Alexei and daughter Ava Mae. —J.C.

STERLING and the distinctive Sterling logo are registered
trademarks of Sterling Publishing Co., Inc.

Library of Congress Cataloging-in-Publication Data

Chassé, Jill D.
The babysitter's survival guide : fun games, cool crafts, and how to be the
best babysitter in town / Jill D. Chassé ; illustrated by Jessica Secheret.
p. cm.
Includes bibliographical references and index.
ISBN 978-1-4027-4654-3 (hc-plc concealed spiral : alk. paper)
1. Babysitting--Handbooks, manuals, etc. I. Secheret, Jessica. II. Title.
HQ769.5.C53 2010
649.10248--dc22

2009002538

Lot#:
2 4 6 8 10 9 7 5 3 1
04/10

Published by Sterling Publishing Co., Inc.
387 Park Avenue South, New York, NY 10016
© 2010 by Jill D. Chassé
Illustrations © 2010 by Jessica Secheret
Distributed in Canada by Sterling Publishing
c/o Canadian Manda Group, 165 Dufferin Street
Toronto, Ontario, Canada M6K 3H6
Distributed in the United Kingdom by GMC Distribution Services
Castle Place, 166 High Street, Lewes, East Sussex, England BN7 1XU
Distributed in Australia by Capricorn Link (Australia) Pty. Ltd.
P.O. Box 704, Windsor, NSW 2756, Australia

Printed in China

Sterling ISBN 978-1-4027-4654-3

For information about custom editions, special sales, premium and
corporate purchases, please contact Sterling Special Sales
Department at 800-805-5489 or specialsales@sterlingpublishing.com.

Designed by Celia Fuller and Kate Moll

CONTENTS

CHAPTER 1

How to Run Your Business

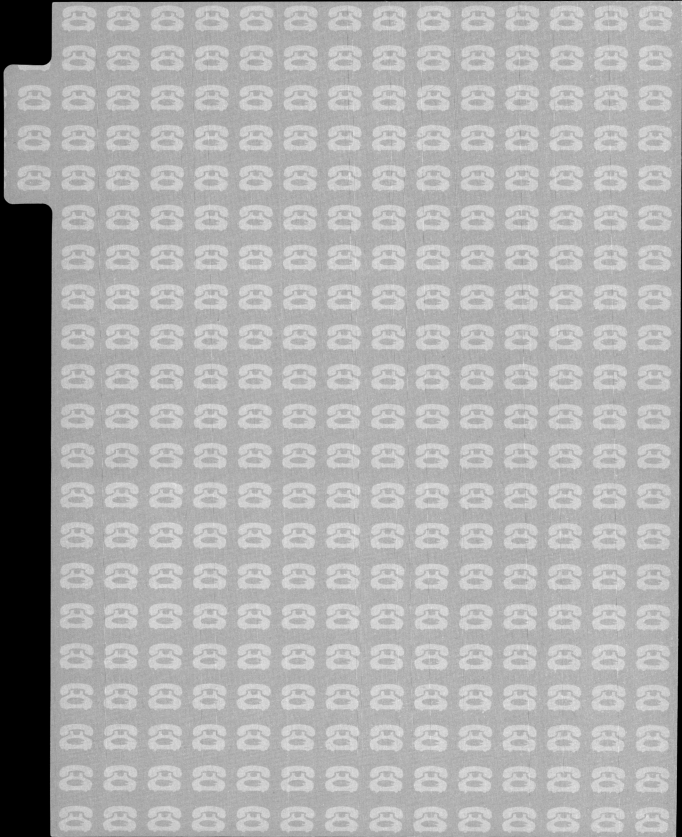

Is Babysitting Right for Me?

I like kids. I need money. I want to babysit! How do I find jobs? Babysitting, like any other job, takes some work to find. It is important to market yourself for the type of babysitting position that you want.

First, decide if you have the skills needed to be a babysitter. A babysitter must be mature, responsible, able to react effectively in case of an emergency, and aware of young children's needs.

If you feel you meet these requirements, determine the age you want to work with. Do you like infants, preschoolers, eight-year-olds? Think about where you have the most experience. Do you have a three-year-old cousin you always watch or a baby sister that you know how to feed and diaper? Make a list of all the experience you have with children. This is going to be your babysitting resume.

Putting Your Resume Together

First things first. Who are you? At the top of the paper, write your name, address, phone number, and e-mail address. This will tell prospective clients not only how to contact you, but how far away from them you live—an important factor if they may have to drive you home after a babysitting job.

Next you should write what is called an objective. This is your goal—what you are looking for in a babysitting job. Your objective should highlight and summarize both your main qualifications and what you are looking for.

Here's an example objective: A position as a babysitter for one to three children, ages six months to five years.

Then you'll want to include a line about when you're available.

For example: Available Monday–Thursday, 3–8 PM; Friday and Saturday nights, 4–midnight.

Next, list your experience. Be sure to put the dates first!

Here's an example: May 2005–September 2007: Babysat for my three cousins, currently ages three, five, and eight. Designed art projects and spent afternoons in the park.

Finally, you need references. Your references may be parents you babysat for in the past or teachers who know you well. Whomever you decide on, make sure to ask first if they would mind being contacted. Getting permission is very important, and you're more likely to get a good recommendation from someone who has had time to think about it and prepare.

If you know your references are busy, you may want to ask them for a prewritten reference letter. Be sure to make copies of all your reference letters and share them with potential clients.

If you are unable to get a reference letter, you should ask your references to be available by e-mail or phone. If they have agreed to be available by phone, find out what the best hours are to reach them.

Encourage your references to mention the following:

- How they know/knew you (a neighbor, a client, or a teacher)
- How long they have known you ("since summer of 2005" or "for four years")
- Positive qualities demonstrated in the capacity in which they knew you (taught kids new songs, helped baby learn to walk, etc.).

Some of your references may ask that you not include their information on your resume, but rather provide it only to people who ask for it. If this occurs, you may want to write "references available upon request" on your resume and create a separate reference sheet to hand out if you are asked for it. If you do create a separate sheet, be sure to include your own contact information at the top. That way if it gets separated from your resume, the potential client will still know whose references they have.

Whether you include references on your resume or on a separate sheet, the information you provide will be the same: the name of your reference, phone number and/or e-mail address, the ages of the children you watched (if the reference is a client), and the dates of employment (again, if the reference is a client; if not, include how the person knows you and how long they have known you). It's also a good idea to include the address of any previous client who is serving as a reference. This will tell the parents what neighborhoods you have worked in and are familiar with.

Here's a sample entry:

Mr. and Mrs. Smith
634 Cranberry Lane
Willard, NY 10362
(827) 555-9776
Ages of children: currently two and four
Dates employed: summer of 2010

Be sure to carry extra copies of your resume and reference sheet with you whenever you go on an interview.

On the next page you'll find a sample of a completed resume.

Resume

Joey A. Lopez
123 Pine Drive,
Cedar, NJ 07019
(973) 555-4567
JALsitter@email.com

OBJECTIVE

A position as a babysitter for one to three children, ages six months to five years

EXPERIENCE

May 2009–September 2010: Babysat for my three cousins, currently ages three, five, and eight. Designed art projects and spent afternoons in the park.

Summer 2010: Babysat for Smith children

REFERENCES

Mr. and Mrs. Smith
634 Cranberry Lane
Willard, NY 10362
(827) 555-9776
Ages of children: currently two and four
Date employed: Summer of 2010

Determining Your Rates

Before you can go into business, you need to decide what to charge for your services. The going rate is anywhere from minimum wage up to twice that amount, depending on your qualifications and the area you live in.

First Aid/CPR

If you plan to do a lot of babysitting, it would be a good idea to take a CPR and basic first aid class. You'll be more confident when it comes to watching children, parents will trust you more, and you may even be able to charge more for your services.

Many high schools, local fire departments, and hospitals have classes that are not too expensive and provide you with knowledge of these lifesaving techniques. The American Red Cross also provides a babysitting course that will further your knowledge of how to take care of children.

You can even keep your course completion certificate in the pocket in the back of this book!

So what are your qualifications? Have you been babysitting for years? Can you get yourself to and from a babysitting job? Have you taken a babysitting course or a first aid/CPR class? These are all important factors and can bump up your asking price.

But they aren't the only factors to consider. Will you charge more for babysitting multiple children or for taking care of a baby? Is there an extra charge if the parents are out beyond your regular hours of availability?

You don't have to advertise all of these factors, just choose a rate that sounds reasonable based on your experience, but be prepared to discuss rates with potential clients during the interview.

Before deciding on your final rate, be sure to look at other advertisements that are up in your neighborhood. You may think that you're worth $10 an hour, but you don't want to lose the job because everyone else is charging only $6. Remember, babysitting is a business, and it pays to be competitive.

Advertising Your New Business

Now that you're prepared to impress parents with your professional resume and you've set your rates, it's time to let your customers know that you're out there. The best way to do that is with flyers or business cards. But what should you put on your advertisements?

First, and most important, list your name, phone number, and e-mail address so that potential clients know how to contact you. Then provide your hours of availability and the base rate you have decided to charge. It would also be a good idea to include your age so that parents can decide if you are old enough to watch their children.

If you're creating a flyer, you may also want to include a line or two about your experience. For example, "I have been babysitting for five years" or "I have CPR training." Anything that sets you apart from the other babysitters who are advertising their services is a plus.

And finally, be sure to include a headline that will quickly allow parents to see what kind of job you are seeking. "Babysitter" or "Babysitting Service" will get the point across nicely.

Business cards provide you with less space to get across your information, so you'll have to choose the truly important facts. To create your own business card, see the following pages titled "Make Your Own Business Cards!" Your actual experience with children is the strongest information you can share with a parent, so list this first. This shows that you not only have the knowledge and experience, but also that you have enjoyed your time with kids enough to want to do it again and again! Always be sure to include your name and contact information, as well as the headline "Babysitter" or "Babysitting Service." If you have the room, you can include one additional fact from your flyer.

Make Your Own Business Cards!

Use the perforated cards on this page to make your own business cards that you can distribute to potential clients. The top line is for your name—be sure to write your full name. There is also room for your telephone number and e-mail address, so people know how to contact you. You can also decorate your business cards however you like, but do not draw over the important information!

Babysitting Service

_____
name

_____
telephone

_____
e-mail address

Babysitting Service

_____
name

_____
telephone

_____
e-mail address

Babysitting Service

_____
name

_____
telephone

_____
e-mail address

Babysitting Service

_____
name

_____
telephone

_____
e-mail address

Babysitting Service

_____
name

_____
telephone

_____
e-mail address

Babysitting Service

_____
name

_____
telephone

_____
e-mail address

Where Should I Put My Signs?

Once you've put together your marketing materials, you're ready to advertise and get a job!

Local libraries, food stores, and community playgrounds are all excellent places to put up your flyers. Parents visit these locations often and are likely to see your advertisement. Local elementary schools and camps are also good places to post flyers, especially near the area where parents wait to pick up their kids. Remember to ask permission before you post your flyer! The last thing you want is to get in trouble for posting your flyers somewhere they shouldn't be.

Another good place to advertise is in the local or community papers. Some newspapers offer free or cheap classified ads that will really help you get the word out there.

And finally, don't forget how important word-of-mouth is. Ask the parents you already babysit for to recommend you to their friends. You may even want to ask them if they will take a few of your business cards to hand out to other parents in need of a babysitter.

CHAPTER 2
The Interview

Get A Job!

You've set up your resume, put up a flyer, and received a phone call! Mr. and Mrs. Clark want to talk to you about watching little Jessica. Don't get nervous! As long as you are comfortable, prepared, honest, and presentable, you'll do great!

The most important thing you can do on an interview is to make a good impression. This is your chance to prove that the parents can trust you with their children. So here are a few things to remember:

- Arrive on time
- Introduce yourself in a courteous manner
- Wear something clean, presentable, and professional. It should be something that you feel comfortable in, but that isn't too revealing or inappropriate. It should be something similar to what you'd wear when babysitting.

Remember that although the decision to hire you rests with the parents, this is as much your interview as it is theirs. It is your chance to decide if you feel comfortable working for this family, so ask questions. Find out the important information up front:

How many children will you be watching and how old are they?

Do any of the children have special needs?

What days and hours will they want you to babysit?

How will you get home after a job?

What qualities are the parents looking for in a babysitter?

Then try to find out something about the children. "Is Jessica involved in any sports?" you can ask. They may say yes, she is on a soccer team. Now you know you can play soccer with her in the backyard and she'll have fun!

Use the child's name and ask things that are helpful and appropriate. Show a genuine interest and learn as much as you can about the child. The parents know more than anyone else about their children. They will tell you important information that you wouldn't otherwise know, like the fact that their daughter always cries when they leave but her special teddy bear will cheer her up, or the fact that their son will say he's allowed to play ball in the house, but that's not actually true.

Once you've learned what you can about the children, get to know the parents and what they're okay with. How would they feel about you bringing crafts and activities? Is there anything they would like you to avoid while they are in their home? Perhaps they would prefer that you not go into the basement or answer the phone. It's important to ask so you'll know your boundaries.

Talk about your strengths and experience, but don't become self-absorbed or self-conscious. Be sure to keep your attention on the job and the child, not on yourself. For example, you may say: "I have been babysitting for three years and I just love interacting with children. Last year I took a water safety class, so I feel comfortable taking children to the pool."

Be prepared to talk about the following points. Even if the parents don't ask, they are great things to discuss and show how prepared and experienced you are:

> Talk about your CPR and/or first aid training.
>
> If you can swim, let the parents know. This is great for summer babysitting and it will make parents who have a pool feel more comfortable.
>
> Can you drive? Do you have a car? Have you driven children in it (and do you feel comfortable driving children)? How's your driving record?
>
> How well do you know your way around the area? If it's very well, tell them. It's good for parents to know you won't get lost with the kids if you go out of the house or neighborhood for a walk or drive if they approve those activities.
>
> Sometimes parents ask you to do some household tasks like laundry, dishes, shopping, cooking for children, etc. If this is okay with you, let them know. If not, it shouldn't interfere with babysitting, but you should tell them.
>
> Be sure to mention if you have any issues with pets or allergies.

After discussing the job, parents may ask about your rate. Be prepared to tell them what you charge per hour (or if you have a flat rate for the evening) and any special charges that you might need to include, such as, an extra dollar an hour for two kids instead of one, or extra for doing household tasks. This is also a good time to discuss how the parents plan to pay you (cash or check; after the job or before, if you charge a flat fee).

When the interview is over, remember to thank the parents and tell them you look forward to hearing from them.

Beyond Regular Babysitting

Some parents like to do co-op babysitting or nanny-shares with their friends. How comfortable are you with occasional doubling up or watching kids from two or three families? Do you have experience with watching several children at once?

At times parents may also ask you to go on vacation with them. Vacation babysitting can be a fun and rewarding experience. It gives parents some free time, and makes time together with the family less stressful since a babysitter can give them a hand. It's also a chance for you to relax a little and get away while getting paid and doing what you enjoy. If this is something that interests you, let them know.

Pricing for vacation babysitting may run a little differently than your typical evening at their home. Some parents will offer a flat rate for a trip, others will continue to pay hourly. A suggestion for a vacation price would be to take your hourly rate and multiply it by 8 hours each day. For example, if you are making $8 an hour, that would be $64 a day. If you take a trip with a family for 3 days, the total would be $192. You might not work a full 8-hour shift like you would at a store or office, but the cost analysis is about the same.

When you're planning to go on vacation with a family, make sure you discuss break times and free time for yourself. Before you agree to go, ask the parents what hours they expect you to be available to watch the kids. Also, find out if you will be on your own for meals or if you'll be eating with the family. If they are paying for your meals, lodging, and /or travel, you might consider charging them less for babysitting.

Things to Look Out for

The family you are meeting with will most often set the place for the interview. An interviewer should never take advantage of you. This includes asking you to have alcohol, making sexual advances, or suggesting a relationship or activity that is unprofessional. An interview should always take place in an appropriate setting, such as the living room or kitchen, not in a bar or bedroom. If the family suggests meeting in a place that does not feel right to you, it is okay to tell them that you don't feel comfortable with the choice and suggest an alternate location. If you do feel that an interviewer is taking advantage of you, politely excuse yourself and tell an adult.

CHAPTER 3

Getting the Information You Need

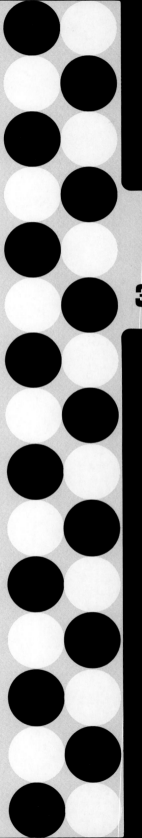

3

Dressing the Part

The interview went well and you got the job! Now what?
When you go on a babysitting job, you should wear something that looks presentable and appropriate, but that will allow you to be active and play with the kids. This means no sweats or ripped T-shirts—old or torn clothing is not respectable to the parents. This also means no stockings and heels. It's difficult to run after a two-year-old with stilettos, and someone is bound to get hurt!

Remember that you're probably going to get dirty, so don't wear your favorite cashmere sweater or new dress slacks. Try jeans or khakis with a polo or nice shirt. Don't wear dangling earrings when watching a child younger than two— they'll look like a fantastic toy to grab! The harder it is to pull on your clothing, the better off everyone will be.

Making a Good Impression

If you are being picked up by one of the parents, be sure you are ready to go at least ten minutes before the time discussed. If you're driving yourself or getting dropped off, arrive at the house on time. If this is your first time at that home, give yourself an extra ten to fifteen minutes to do a walk-through with the parents and become familiar with where things are.

If the children will be asleep for some of the time you're babysitting, bring something to do with you. This is true of most night jobs. If you're watching a three-year-old from 5 to 10 PM, expect to play with the child until about eight. After that, you'll need to be prepared with homework, a laptop, or a book to read. It makes an especially good impression to bring homework or study materials, but remember to bring them out only after the kids are put to bed, not when you should be watching them. It's fine to watch TV after the kids are asleep, but only if you get the parents' permission first.

What Should You Know Before a Parent Leaves You Alone?

The most important thing about babysitting is to keep the children safe. This is essentially your main purpose. Entertainment and education are always secondary to SAFETY. Children need supervision at all times! You are fully responsible for the children when the parents are not there.

When you are in a new place, make sure you know the address. Have it written down where you can access it in the case of an emergency. Even if you know it by heart, write it down anyway. It is easy to forget when you're in a panic during an emergency situation. Also be sure to write down the family's name, children's names, nearest cross street, instructions on how to contact the parents, emergency phone numbers such as 911 in the U.S. and Canada for your local police and fire department, the hospital, the numbers of close relatives and neighbors, the doctor's name and phone number along with a medical release, and the U.S. National Poison Control Center, which is 800-222-1222. At the back of this book you'll find card Emergency Information Sheets, which are for writing down all of this information. Fill out the left-hand cards to keep in this book and ask the parents if you can tear out the duplicate from the right side of the page to keep somewhere in the house where you'll have easy access to it.

In addition to this information, which you'll want every time you babysit, find out where the parents will be, how to contact them there, and when they are expected home.

Child Information Sheet

You should also ask the parent to go over the child's medical information with you. Is the child taking any medicine? If so, make certain you know how much and when it should be given. If you do have to give the medicine to the child, write down what you gave and when so the parent will know. Does the child have any allergies (particularly food allergies) that you should be aware of? Are there any other diet restrictions? As you gather information on the child you are watching, enter it into a child information sheet, like the ones provided at the back of this book. This sheet contains not only important medical information, but a list of the child's likes and dislikes as well. As with the Emergency Information Sheets, you would fill out one card to keep in this book and tear out the duplicate card on the right side of the page to keep at the house where you are babysitting.

Remember, it's a lot easier to have fun with someone who knows you. Kids may be small, but they have their own personalities, likes and dislikes, preferences, and ideas. As their babysitter, it's important you know the little ins and outs of their personality so that both of you will enjoy your time together.

Many of a child's favorites can be learned through communication with the parents, which is why it's important to go over the child information sheet before they leave. As you learn things like a favorite toy, movie, character, TV show, book, or song, add this information to the child's information sheet. Remember to make a different sheet for each of the kids you babysit for, and update it as you learn more about the child's likes and dislikes. The sheet is a good reference guide and will serve as a nice refresher the next time you babysit for the family.

The Walk-through

Before the parents leave, do a walk-through of the house. Look for potential hazards in the home such as open stairways, uncovered electrical outlets, and sharp objects that are within reach. Find out where the parents keep the cleaning supplies and chemicals so you can keep the kids away from them, and locate the first aid supplies in case someone *does* get hurt. (If this happens, make sure you wash out all cuts before you put a bandage on, and use antibacterial cream if the parents say that is okay.) Ask about candles and flashlights, as well, in case of a blackout while the parents are gone.

Find out what the fire escape plan is. If there isn't one, be sure you know ALL the exits from the home. Is there a back door? A porch? How would you exit from upstairs? Also, ask where the smoke alarms and fire extinguishers are. If you don't know how to use the fire extinguisher, have an adult show you before you are alone in the house with the children.

House Rules

Once you've finished the walk-through, be sure to go over the house rules for both you and the children. You need to know what the rules are so that you can comply and make sure the children are doing what they are supposed to do. House rules

Fire Safety

Once the parents leave, practice fire safety with the children. Determine a designated meeting place outside the house that both you and the children know about if you lose track of one another inside during a fire. If the child is old enough to walk, tell him to GET OUT, DO NOT HIDE, and meet at the special spot.

Inside you can practice staying LOW to the ground, feeling a door for heat BEFORE opening it, and STOPPING, DROPPING, AND ROLLING if any part of them catches on fire.

If there IS a fire in the house:

➡ YELL "FIRE" as loud as you can, and gather the children.

➡ GET OUT of the house—don't try to put out the fire. Go to the designated meeting spot if everyone is not with you. Once you have all the children, go to a neighbor's house and call 911.

➡ Don't go back inside!

can be simple tasks like taking off your shoes when you come inside, shutting all the doors in the house when the air conditioning is on, or never putting your feet up on the couch. These rules are important to a family and a household, so it's best to learn and respect them when you are a guest in their house. Some of the more common ones include:

HOMEWORK

If the child is old enough to have homework, there are usually a lot of rules associated with this task. Does he have to finish it before playing? Does she get to do her homework at the kitchen table or does it have to be in her room? Parents usually have these rules locked in, so just ask if there are any homework rules and they'll let you know.

TELEVISION

You'll probably run into television rules no matter what age the child is. Generally, parents don't want their babies to be stuck in front of a TV and may bring up this point. There are some infant/toddler video programs that a family may approve. If this is the case, they'll probably tell you about the video or DVD and show you where it is. Remember not to over-stimulate the baby with the television. Keep him in front of it for only a short period of time and always be there to supervise!

As children get older, they may want to watch a TV program or special show. Toddlers can be very vocal and direct in voicing their opinion and choices in television. Ask the parents directly whether

the child can watch TV, what he or she can watch, and for how long. Also find out when the child can watch TV. Maybe he is allowed one video before bed or can't watch anything on TV after 7 PM. The parents are ultimately responsible for setting time limits, schedules, and restrictions for viewing, but as the babysitter it's up to you to enforce those rules.

You should also be sure to find out what your own TV privileges are. Are you allowed to watch the television? Would parents prefer that you only do so once the children are soundly asleep? This is a good time to find out about your other privileges as well. Are you allowed to use the computer? Can you eat the chips that are in the kitchen? Make sure you know so that you don't overstep your boundaries.

USING THE TELEPHONE

Are you allowed to answer the phone? If so, how should you answer, "Smith residence" or simply "hello"? Is it okay for you to use the phone to make local calls? If so, remember not to offer any information on the phone and not to tell anyone you're alone. Also check to see if the child is allowed to answer and/or use the phone. This is especially applicable for older elementary-school kids who tend to use the phone when their parents are home.

If you *are* allowed to use the phone, be sure you're not talking on the phone instead of watching and playing with the kids. Remember, you're not getting paid to talk to your friends.

If you have a cell phone, be sure the parents have the number to reach you in case of a power outage.

ANSWERING THE DOOR

Find out if the parents are expecting anyone to stop by. Next ask them if they have a procedure for answering the door or rules they want you to follow (such as looking through the window first or not opening the door after 9 PM).

At the End of the Job

PAYMENT

Before the parents come home, figure out how much they owe you for your services. Be prepared to make change for them if need be.

If the parents arrive home and say they can't pay you, it is important that you first ask them why they are not paying you. Do they not have money with them? Do they plan to pay you the next time you babysit? If the parents say that they have to pay you another time, ask for an IOU. A written and signed note would qualify.

If they still do not pay you, talk to your parents. It is also helpful to have another adult present when you speak to your employer about the situation. The parents hired you with the understanding that they would pay you at the end of the job. If they repeatedly fail to do so, you should terminate your relationship.

WHAT IF THE PARENTS ARE LATE COMING HOME?

Sometimes parents show up late because of circumstances beyond their control. If it's more than fifteen minutes past the time they told you they would be home, you should give them a call on the phone number they left for you (fifteen to twenty minutes is a reasonable amount of time to wait, in case there was traffic or an accident on the route they take home).

If over an hour passes and you can't reach the parents, call the emergency number they left (it may be a neighbor, a family friend, or a relative) and explain the situation to that person. Make sure you also tell *your* parents that your employer is late and that you will be coming home at a later time than expected.

What To Do After the Parents Leave (Safety Tips)

- If it is evening, turn on the porch/outside light, and keep the window shades closed and the doors locked.

- DO NOT open the door for anyone unless you personally know the person. If someone is insisting on coming in and you do not recognize that person, or if you suspect a prowler, DO NOT LET THEM IN, CALL THE POLICE AT 911.

- If the children are awake, know their location at all times and never leave them alone too long.

- Never leave a baby unattended on a changing table, bed, or highchair. Babies don't understand the danger of heights, and once they learn how to roll (about four months old), they keep moving! Babies love to practice their new skills, but they need to practice in a safe place. Even if he can't crawl yet, a baby can easily roll off of a changing table or bed in the second you turn your back. In a highchair, a little squirmer can slither under the tray and fall right onto the floor. To avoid this, use safety straps whenever they are available.

- Never leave a baby unattended in the bathtub. Baths are even more dangerous than changing tables, beds, and highchairs. A child can drown in just an inch of water. Even if it looks like the baby is sitting well in the tub, it only takes a second to slip and go head first into the water.

- Keep a close watch on a baby in a walker. The baby may seem very independent in her walker, but she has no idea if she's headed down the stairs or into the fireplace. It's up to you to keep her out of harm's way and let her practice running those little legs in a risk-free zone, like an open playroom or den with no pointy table edges to run into.

- If for any reason you must leave the house, TAKE THE CHILDREN WITH YOU!

- If the parents have given you permission to take the children out of the house, make sure you have a house key with you when you leave. Double-check that all doors and windows are locked, and have the children go to the bathroom before leaving. This will help to avoid accidents or having to use public restrooms.

- If the children are asleep, check on them about every 15 minutes.

It is okay to ask the parents to give you a call if they are going to be running late. If they are consistently late, you may want to consider not working for them anymore, but remember, be polite and explain the problem you have with their lateness. They may correct this behavior or they may say they will find another sitter. Either way, do your best to stay on good terms. The last thing you want is for them to tell other parents that you were unprofessional.

GETTING HOME

If you do not drive, it is important to find out how you'll be getting back home after your babysitting job. Often, parents will provide this transportation, but don't assume they will drive you. Ask beforehand so you can plan alternate transportation if necessary. Even if you are within walking distance, some parents would rather take you home, especially if the job ends late in the evening. Others will trust you to find your own way home. Whatever the plan, always make sure you have an alternate way to get home.

If the parent agrees to take you home, but appears intoxicated, don't accept a ride with him or her. It is okay to politely refuse and call your backup transportation.

CHAPTER 4

What to Expect from Children of Different Ages

4

Prepare Yourself

Before you're alone with the kids, you should know what to expect. Here's a breakdown of different ages and the behavior you will most likely see, as well as some activities specific to each age group.

Infants (Newborn to One Year)

Babies are not only capable of interacting and playing, they learn and soak up loads of new information to help their brains grow as you play with them. Babies also need a lot of attention. When they cry, there's a reason. It's okay to hold them and pick them up. This is how they learn to trust and learn about the world.

For **newborns**, good activities involve calm and gentle games. During the first month they prefer looking at contrasting colors, like black, white, and red. If the parents don't have any newborn books available, it is nice to bring your own to share and read. Newborns also like mirrors and watching themselves. Music, soft lullabies, and children's songs are great to play for a new baby as well.

At **two months** a baby's vision will allow him to find interest in more colorful and complex pictures and toys. Pick out a book and open it in front of the baby.

Holding a baby

When you pick up an infant from his crib or bassinette, it is VERY IMPORTANT to support the HEAD. Slide one hand under the child's neck and open your fingers so that your hand can support the whole head. Slide your other hand under the baby's lower back or between his legs. This is the hand that will be holding the weight of the baby. The hand under the baby's head is for supporting the neck only. Make sure you are holding the baby around the torso. When your hands feel secure, lift up the infant and hold him close to your body. You may want to practice at home with a doll.

Babies are sensitive and delicate. They need and want to be close to your body. Not only does that give them support, it gives them warmth and a healing human touch. Remember to keep the baby secure as a bundle. Support the head and keep the baby's body upright.

Point out different items and make silly sounds to go with each item, such as "This is a cow—a cow says moooooo!"

At **three months**, babies become more social and interactive. They start to prefer games that involve tugging and grasping. Find a rattle or some other toy that makes a sound. Gently shake the toy near one side of the baby. Then move it around his head and shake it again. Move it slowly from place to place and see if the baby will follow it with his eyes. If he tries to touch the rattle, hold it in reaching distance and help him grasp it by putting it against his palm.

By **four months**, a baby can usually hold up his or her head independently and practice early crawl movements, such as pushing up from a belly position. He may giggle when you tickle him or may take a toy from you. Babies at this age will begin to babble and imitate sounds. Some fun activities you can play with a baby this age include:

TOUCH AND FEEL

Pick up the baby and walk into the living room. Go to the couch and tell him what it is. Next, have him touch it and tell him how it feels (say "soft"). Continue on throughout the room finding other interesting objects and textures. Be careful not to touch anything breakable.

PEEK-A-BOO OBJECT

Get a small bag that you cannot see through. Inside place some of the baby's favorite items. Sit facing the baby and pull the items out one by one. Say, "Look! It's your rattle!" Then hide it again in the bag. Ask the baby, "Where did the rattle go?" Wait a few moments, and then pull out the item again and say "Look! Here is your rattle!" Move on to another item. Do this with three or four items, or until the baby gets bored (looks away, seems disinterested, or starts to fidget or cry).

READING

Reading to a baby at this age helps language skills develop. Board books and those with bright colors are great.

By **five or six months old**, a baby will be able to sit up on his own. Babies at this age can grasp objects and even move them from one hand to the other. Direct interaction occurs more openly now, so talk face-to-face and make lots of facial expressions. Be attentive to the child's moods. Ask him questions like "Do you like this soft ball?" or "Does this applesauce taste sweet?" Use lots of descriptive words (color, taste, size, feel, shape, etc.). Remember to repeat, repeat, repeat. Other fun activities for this age include rolling a soft ball back and forth with the baby; giving the child a toy that rattles, jingles, or rings when you shake it, and making music together (you can shake to a beat or even with some background music); and giving the baby a wet (wrung out, not soaking) washcloth and dry washcloth. Explain the difference *(This is wet—This is dry)* and let him or her feel each one.

Babies at this age also love to use their hands. Hold the baby's hand and show him how to do patty-cake or the Itsy Bitsy Spider. Clap your hands then take the baby's hands and gently clap them together.

Eight to ten months is an exciting time for an infant. A baby at this age is becoming mobile! You'll have to keep up with him or her. Be sure that the parents have the house baby-proofed (covered outlets, locked cabinets, etc.) before you let the child wander. If they do not, you need to be especially cautious of these things.

Try these activities with an eight- to ten-month-old:

TRACING SHAPES

Find a colorful book or magazine. Put the baby on your lap and open up the book. Trace the shapes you find with your finger and describe what you see (for example, trace a beach ball and say "round"). Hold the baby's hand gently and trace the shape with his finger. Repeat twice with each object.

RATTLE DANCE

Turn on some music and get two rattles. Sit on the floor with the baby in front of you and shake the rattle to the beat of the music. Give the baby the other rattle and see if she'll shake it with you.

SOUND HUNT

Take the baby on a walk through the house. Find objects in each room that make noise, and repeat that noise (such as the clock in the bedroom, which makes a tick-tock noise, or the microwave in the kitchen, which makes a beeping sound).

OTHER GOOD ACTIVITIES

Other activities include stacking blocks or containers, scribbling with crayons and paper (another great item to bring if the parents don't have any), or making drums out of upside-down cups and spoons.

Between ten and twelve months, most babies will begin walking. Children at this age can usually recognize objects (*Where is the dog? Bring me Pokie bunny…*). Good activities include using a blanket, cups, or canisters in the playroom to hide some little toys, then asking the children to find them; pushing around toy cars and trucks (only big ones—larger than a toilet paper tube—until the kids are over three); or playing hand rhymes and songs such as "Patty Cake," "The Itsy Bitsy Spider," and "Round and Round the Garden." If you're not familiar with these songs and rhymes, you may find it helpful to get a nursery rhyme or hand rhyme book from the library or bookstore, or watch a few children's shows to learn some fun play songs.

Another fun game to play is "Bicycle Trip": lay the baby on her back and gently bend her little knees, bring them up to her chest and back down again in a bicycle-pedaling motion. Make up a place you're going to ride to and pause pedaling to check out the sights. You could say, for example, "Let's ride our bike to the zoo! Pedal pedal pedal—look at those monkeys! Pedal pedal pedal…*Wow!* Check out the lion! Roar!" Think of all the make-believe places you can go!

At first you may feel silly talking to a baby since they can't talk back and may look confused, but they can hear and process what you're saying in their own way. They will become familiar with your voice and it will increase their security when you babysit again.

Remember that infants can't talk, so they may communicate through crying. Crying can mean that they need a diaper change, they are hungry, or they just want to be held. The more time you spend with the baby, the easier it will be to understand his cues.

Toddlers (Ages 1–2)

Toddlers are called toddlers because they toddle! This is the age when they start to become more independent, not only by learning to walk on their own, but also by making choices in what they want to play, eat, and do. They love to do things all by themselves. It's fun as a babysitter to offer the toddler several choices and let him decide. Let him pick between two games or decide which book he wants to read. At this age children also love to get into everything, so keep an extra close watch on them!

Here are some activities that can keep toddlers entertained:

CEREAL DRAWINGS

Take a handful of small O's or puffed cereal and put it in a bowl on the table. Then get some kid-safe glue, crayons, and paper. Draw any items you can think of with missing circles and have the toddler fill the circles in with cereal. For example, draw some cars without wheels, and have the toddler put the cereal where the wheels would go.

PRETEND PARTY

Get a bunch of stuffed animals together and set up a table in an open play area. Pretend there's a birthday cake in the center of the table, and find "presents" from the child's toy box. Sing "Happy Birthday" to one of the stuffed animals and pretend to blow out candles on a  cake. You can even make party hats and placemats out of construction paper. Toddlers love to color, so they can help to design these!

BLANKET TENT

Pretend you're going camping and make a tent inside the house! Drape a blanket over two chairs or a table. Throw a bunch of stuff inside the tent, such as books, pillows, and stuffed animals. Crawl into the tent with the child and make outdoor sounds, like crickets chirping and owls hooting. If you have a flashlight you can play with, take it into the tent with you and make shadow animals on the walls.

Between **14 and 20 months** of age, a child will usually start to speak. They begin with simple words that they have heard often, such as "mama" or "dada." These words eventually turn into two-word phrases, which is the next step on the journey of speech. Two-word phrases such as "come baby" or "doggie gone" begin around the age of two years. By this point, a baby should have around 50 words in his vocabulary. When a child can link two words together, it shows an understanding of both words and content. Be sure to talk to the child and encourage him to talk back.

Terrible Twos!

When a toddler continually expresses himself in a negative way (bad mood, temper tantrums, etc.), he could be making a statement that he *needs your acknowledgment*. Playing *with* him, not just watching him play, can help to prevent tantrums.

Two-year-old children are active and outgoing and can be a handful, but they are also getting interested in doing more in-depth games and activities. Here are a few you can try!

NUMBER JUMP

Draw big numbers on construction paper. Cut them out and scatter them on the floor in the play area. Call out the numbers and have the child jump onto the paper number when you call it out.

PAPER RACES

Crumple up a bunch of pieces of paper and lay them out on a table. Sit the child at the table with a straw and ask him to blow the paper across the table. You sit across from the child and blow the paper balls back to him.

FREEZE DANCE

Put the radio on and begin to dance. A few minutes after the music starts, yell "freeze" and turn off the music. The child has to stop moving completely in the position he was in when the music stopped. Hold it for a few seconds then turn the music on again. Repeat the freeze every few minutes throughout the song.

COLOR FISH FIND

Cut out a bunch of fish from different colored construction paper. Hide them all around the playroom or child's play area. When all are hidden, ask the child to find a fish then bring it to you and tell you the color. When the child has found all of the fish, line them up and say the colors together.

Preschoolers (Ages 3–4)

At this age, children are little social beings, interested in what everyone's doing and why. The way a child looks at the world and those around him or her has a significant impact on his or her development.

Little girls learn about being female from sisters, aunts, and moms. They watch Mom put on makeup, go to work, or make dinner, and model their behavior and actions from what they see.

Little boys learn how to be male from brothers, uncles, and dads. They watch the guys in their life and pick up on their actions and activities.

Preschoolers will start to copy this behavior and try to be like the grown ups they see. Without a *positive role model,* children may acquire inappropriate behaviors from bad influences in a negative environment. This is why it is so important for you to be a positive role model! They are watching what you do and what you say. Kids at this age also like role-playing and make-believe dress-up games, like putting on heels and a fancy hat to pretend to be Mommy, or wearing Dad's tie and carrying a briefcase, pretending to go to work. Have some dramatic playtime with the child you are watching. Ask what he wants to be, and find something around the house to help him pretend. Enter a make-believe world for a little while and allow the child to take on the part. If he wants to be a doctor, bring him some stuffed animals so he can check their temperatures, or help him put on a bandage. If he wants to be a teacher, set up a pretend classroom with his action figures and give him a few grown-up books so he can pretend he is teaching.

Some other activities you can do with preschool-aged kids include:

ANIMAL CHARADES

Fill a shoebox or paper bag with pictures of animals. Let the child pull out the pictures one at a time and act them out while you guess what he's doing. If there are other kids, let them try to guess what the animal is, too.

GUESS THE OBJECT

Collect a handful of kid-safe objects and put them in a pile on a table or the floor. Then get a small blanket and put it in front of the objects. Ask the child to close his eyes, then hide one of the objects under the blanket. Let the child feel the object under the blanket and try to determine what it is. If he can't guess it, give him easy hints *(It's red, it goes fast)* until he figures it out.

ANIMAL RACES

Go into a wide open space where it's okay to run around, like a playroom or backyard. Make a start and finish line, marked by a chair or stuffed animal. Put the child at the start and name an animal. The child then has to act like that animal all the way to the finish line. This one is great with more than one child, too. Remember to allow all the kids a chance to win. Some good animals for this game are turtles *(Can you crawl slowly?)*, bunnies *(Hop! Hop! Hop!)*, elephants *(Let me see that trunk!)*, and bats *(Flap those wings!)*. Think of animals that don't go too fast to reduce the risk of accidents!

GROCERY STORE

Pick some items from the kitchen and put them in a bag (not refrigerated stuff, which might go bad if you're playing for a long time). Have the child go behind a table like it's a checkout counter and come up to the counter with the items. Pretend to "check out" and ask how much each object is. Then ask the child "What can I do with this one?" If the child can't think of anything, give him some suggestions *(Can I make anything with it? Can I cook it?)*.

Early Elementary School (Age 5-7)

A younger child believes that rules are set in stone and cannot be altered. Older children understand that rules are developed by people, not some all-powerful force, and can be changed or amended. More important, they aren't afraid to test the rules. They also aren't afraid to tell you how they feel and express their joy or anger in having a babysitter. Be ready for this, and make sure to enforce the rules their parents set forth, no matter what the children might say.

Older kids often spend time with a group of similar kids going through similar experiences, such as a new baby sister or brother, Miss Jones's third-grade art class, or growth spurts. This peer group takes on a special significance. It offers a place between the world of grown-ups and that of babies. This is important for you, the babysitter, to understand, so you know what to talk to them about. Ask them questions about their friends, school subjects, or TV shows they like to watch. Talk about when you were in first grade or second grade and what you remember about your favorite teacher, class, or friend.

Kids at this age are curious and intelligent enough to sit and learn, yet still very restless and fidgety, so it's good to have some activities planned for them. Some activities for this age are:

MIRRORING
In this game, the child will copy the movements you make. Face each other in a safe, open area. Start slowly by making a movement with a hand or foot. The child should mimic the exact thing you do as you do it as if she's looking in a mirror. After a few movements, switch so that you mirror the child's movements.

MY FAVORITE THINGS

Gather some old magazines and have the child pick out about ten favorite things he finds in the pages. Help him cut out the objects, then take a sheet of paper and help him make a collage by gluing the pictures onto the paper. Have some markers or crayons available if the child wants to add to the collage with some drawings.

COUNTING GAME

At this age kids are really getting into numbers and counting. Write the numbers one through ten on a card or piece of paper. Leave a blank space next to each number. Go around the house with the child (outside, too, if the weather's nice) and find something to represent each number, such as one clock, two pillows on the couch, three pens on Mommy's desk, etc. until you get to ten.

Mid-Elementary School (Age 8–10)

Children at this age typically spend a lot of time socializing with their friends, whether at their own house or someone else's. When babysitting, find out *exactly* where the child is supposed to be and at what time. If he is not home from school within fifteen minutes of the expected time, call one of the parents.

You should also make sure you know what the rules are for going to friends' houses or having friends over. Know what the child is doing and with whom at *all times*. The parents should tell you which friends the child is allowed to play with. Even if the child you are babysitting is with a friend, you are still responsible for him while you are there. If the playdate is at the house you're babysitting in, you need to be involved and supervise the children.

Sometimes the parents will set up a playdate that you do not have to attend. In a situation like this, your responsibility is to get the child to and from the event safely and on time. Find out who you need to drop the child off with, such as an adult contact at the playdate, party, or event. Leave the child only with that adult. Give the adult your contact information and stay nearby in case there is a problem and the child needs to be picked up early. The adult should also have the contact information of the child's parents.

When it is time to pick up the child, arrive on time and ask the responsible adult how the event went. Be sure to find out what the child ate and if there were any problems or injuries.

Know that you are in charge, and don't be afraid to state the rules and give consequences, as long as the parents explain what the punishments and rules are. But remember, children are people, too. Lay down the rules, but do your best to provide an enjoyable environment for a child. Fill the time with enjoyable activities and the children will want to behave for you.

Here are examples of things you can try with school-age kids:

ILLUSTRATOR

Read a chapter of a book and have the child draw a picture or several pictures of the events going on as you read.

TREASURE MAP

Pick an object from the child's toys to hide. Don't choose something that is very small—you don't want it to be too hard to find. Have the child wait in his room while you hide the object. Then sit with him and draw a "treasure map" of the house. Mark the spot where the toy is hidden with an X.

Give the child the map and let him walk through the house trying to follow your directions to find the "treasure."

SHARING ROCK

This is more of a talking game, but it's a great one when you have several kids, especially girls who love to chat. Write down the following open-ended questions on a sheet of paper, or make up your own. Find a clean, smooth stone. Sit in a circle with the kids, holding the rock. Chant "The sharing rock goes round and round, so pass it quickly through the crowd. If you're the one to hold it last, it's time for you to SHARE!" Everyone says "share" loudly, and whoever has the rock at that time answers one of the questions on the list.

- I feel happy when…
- One of my favorite activities is…
- If I won a million dollars, I would…
- When I grow up, I want to…
- One day I hope to travel to…
- If I were a crayon, I would be…
- My favorite vacation was…
- I get really mad when…
- If I had one superpower, it would be…

CHAPTER 5
Comforting Kids

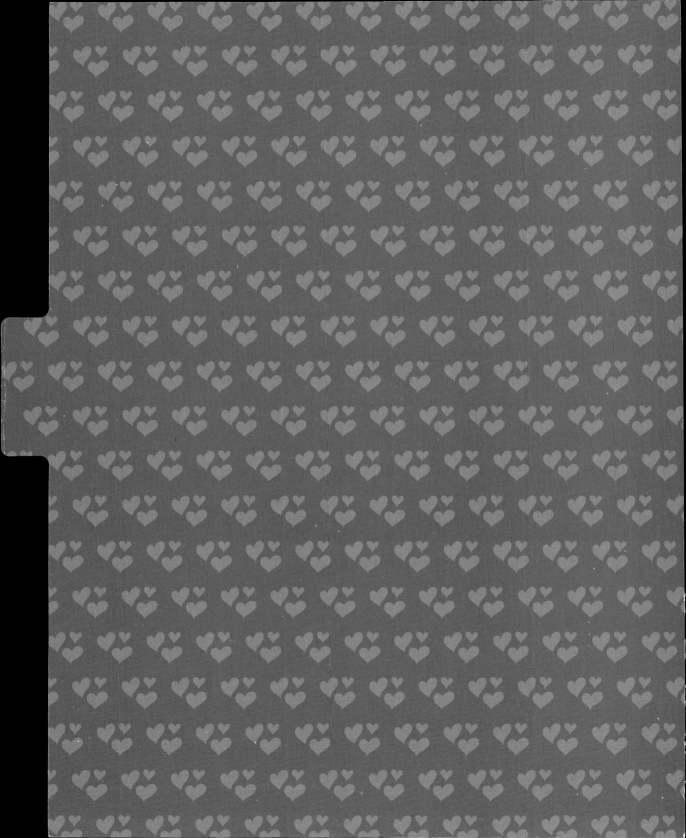

Once Mom and Dad Leave

No matter how happy the children you're watching generally are, there's always the chance that something will upset them and they'll need to be comforted. For younger children, this is particularly true when their parents leave the house. The absence of the child's parents may cause a lot of anxiety, and she may become angry, sad, or scared. Separation anxiety usually begins around age one. Before that, babies will generally take to babysitters or other caregivers pretty well, as long as they are given the attention and necessities they desire for comfort. As children approach one year old, they begin to realize that Mom or Dad is disappearing from their sight, but can't yet grasp that parents will come back. This generally causes lots of tears.

The best way to deal with this is to let the parent kiss or hug the child goodbye, explain they will be back, and walk out. This should be a consistent pattern every time the parent leaves. There's no need to hide or trick the child, which will just cause more fear and confusion when he realizes Mom is gone. Let them have a quick goodbye, then take the child to a favorite activity and start to play.

Don't bring up the parents, but if a child asks about them, be direct and consistent. For example, you can say "Mommy and Daddy went out to dinner but they will be back later. You'll see them in the morning."

Of course, this isn't the only time the child may be upset, so what can you do to help? First, stay calm. A child will pick up on your tension and anxiety and it will usually make things worse. Next, assess the situation. What is making the child cry? Is she hurt? Is she scared? If you did not see an incident occur, ask the child to tell you what hurts or why she is crying. Finally, take action to solve the problem. If it is a first aid issue, follow the first aid procedures on the opposite page and remember to keep talking to the child the whole time with supportive and caring words, like "You are so brave!" If it's an emotional issue, *try to put yourself in the child's shoes*. Say the little girl you're babysitting dropped her doll in the sand. What would make you feel better if you were her? Pick up the doll, clean it off, and make a pretend ice pack. Always remember to give encouraging, supportive, and caring words to the child. Never tell the child not to cry, and don't say "You're such a baby!" These words are hurtful and can make a child feel even worse. Children will usually express their emotions loudly, and cry when they are in pain or frightened, and that's a good thing. Holding emotions inside is not healthy. If the crying goes on for a while, you can

say something like "It's okay, you don't have to cry. You can smile, because I'm here for you."

It's okay to say positive things, like "You've got a lot of courage," but don't say negative and accusing things, like "You're such a coward!"

The attention paid to a child during times of stress and anxiety is *very important*. You can always give her a hug and a smile to help her make it "all better."

First Aid

Accidents can happen at any time, no matter how cautious a babysitter you are. The important thing is that you know how to treat minor injuries when they occur. Below you'll find tips on the best way to deal with a variety of situations.

CUTS/SCRAPES: If a child has a small cut or scrape, the first thing you'll want to do is stop the bleeding. Use a clean cloth or gauze and apply gentle pressure to the cut. Small cuts should stop bleeding on their own. After the bleeding slows and stops, rinse the wound and then wash it gently with soap and water. Do not use any ointments, gels or lotions unless instructed to by the parents. Cover the cut with a clean bandage or gauze. Make sure the bandage stays clean and dry.

BUMPS/BRUISES: If the child has a bump or a bruise, wrap some ice cubes in a washcloth, hand towel, or two paper towels, and have the child hold the ice to the bruised area. If the injury was to the child's head, watch for vomiting, nausea, or dizziness. If you see any of these signs, call 911 and report a head injury.

BURNS: Run the burned area under cool water. Do not apply any creams or ointments. If the burn has large blisters and the skin becomes raised, call 911.

NOSEBLEEDS: Have the child sit up straight and tilt his head slightly forward. Squeeze the child's nostrils for about fifteen minutes. If bleeding does not stop after that time, or gets worse, call 911.

BUG BITES AND STINGS: Apply ice, wrapped in a cloth or towel, to an itch or a painful sting. If you notice anything more than a little red mark (such as dizziness, trouble breathing, a rash, or redness spreading across the skin), call 911.

SPLINTERS: If the splinter is sticking out enough to grab on to, have the child sit in a comfortable place and be very still (putting on a video or TV show often helps with this).

Clean a pair of tweezers with alcohol and wipe dry with a clean cloth. Under a light, grasp the piece that is sticking out and pull quickly. Wash the area and cover with a Band-Aid. If the splinter is embedded under the skin, wash the area gently and inform the parents.

VOMITING: There are many reasons for vomiting. If the child has just eaten before running, jumping, and playing, his food may not be digested yet. See if he has a fever, dizziness, or stomach pains. If he has any of these signs of illness, call the parents and have the child lay down on his side in his bed to rest. It is important he stays on his side so he won't choke if he throws up again. Put a bucket or a big bowl by the side of his bed. If he won't stop vomiting, call 911.

CHOKING: First talk to the child and see if he can cough, breathe, cry, or speak. If he can, encourage him to cough. This may get the item out of the child's throat. Do not attempt any first aid if the child can cough. If he can't cough or make any sound at all, begin first aid for choking. Perform the Heimlich maneuver on the child until the object comes out and he can cough.

To perform the Heimlich maneuver, stand behind the child. Wrap your arms around his waist and lean him slightly forward. Make a fist with your right hand. Position it slightly above the child's belly button. Hold your fist with your other hand and push hard into the child's tummy with a quick, upward thrust.

Choking hazards include grapes, nuts, hard candy, hot dogs, popcorn, balloons, buttons, jewelry, coins, marbles, Legos, and other small toys.

STRAINS OR SPRAINS: A good way to remember how to treat a sprain is by using the acronym **RICE**:

Rest! Do not put any weight or pressure on the injured area.

Ice should be applied to the injured area for twenty to thirty minutes. After this time, take off the ice and reapply it every two hours.

Compress the injury with a bandage or wrap. Don't wrap it too tightly. It should fit like a snug glove.

Elevate the injured body part above the child's heart.

It's not easy for a child to stay still very long, so while he's sitting with ice on the injury, go around the house collecting fun things for him to do while sitting, such as coloring books, puzzles, a video game, or other favorite activities.

In all cases, if the injury seems severe, or the symptoms don't go away, call 911. It's better to be overly cautious than to ignore an injury that could turn serious. And remember to tell the parents if the child has an injury, even one as small as a paper cut. You never know if a tiny cut could get infected or a bump on the head could turn out to be worse than it seems at the time.

Although these basic steps are important, the best way to soothe children of different ages varies. Here are some tips to help make your attempt a bit smoother:

Infants

Unlike an older child, a baby can't tell you why she's crying, so you'll have to use your senses and do some babysitting detective work to figure it out and solve the issue.

First and foremost, check over the whole child to see if there are any obvious problems, such as a diaper pin stuck in her side or a finger pinched in a toy. If there is something injuring the child, remedy it immediately and refer back to your first aid training. As always, make sure you give the parents a full report about the injury when they get home. You might be afraid they will be angry, but not telling them is much worse. They are most concerned about the safety and well-being of their child, so explaining what happened and how you helped will ease their anxiety and concern. Your honesty will also make them feel better about leaving their child in your care again.

If the child appears to be unharmed physically, check to see if she has a wet or dirty diaper. Even if you just changed it, a baby might go again and be uncomfortable, especially if she has diaper rash.

Think about the baby's feeding schedule. Is it near or past a feeding time? If the baby is crying, maybe she is just hungry and letting you know how uncomfortable an empty belly is. If she's already eaten, she may have a bubble in her tummy. Try to gently but firmly burp her. Hold her with her head over your shoulder or lay her face-down over your knees and rub and pat her back softly until she lets out a burp. Keep a burp rag or hand towel on your shoulder in case she spits up. You can also sit her on your lap, and with one hand supporting her chin (not her head) gently pat her back with the other. This method takes a bit more control and practice but often helps the baby burp faster.

Another reason the baby might be crying is that she has been up for a long time, and may need a nap. Try putting her down to sleep; bounce, rock, and soothe the little one into a peaceful nap.

If the baby is not hurt, hungry, or tired, here are some other suggestions to help calm a little one:

RHYTHMIC MOVEMENT

Rocking, calm bouncing, and swinging are all good ways to calm a crying child. Remember, NEVER shake a baby! If you are trying to calm down a crying baby in your arms and get so aggravated at the screaming that you think you might shake too hard, put the baby down in a safe place while you calm down.

How to Change a Baby's Diaper

Dirty diapers can be very uncomfortable for a baby, so it's important that you check them regularly, especially when the baby wakes up from a nap. And remember, babies have sensitive skin, so be sure to wash your hands before you start changing the diaper.

When you're ready, take the baby to the changing area. If there is not a specific changing area, gather the supplies you'll need first (clean diaper, wipes or a wet rag, powder, lotion or ointment, and changing pad). If the parents do not have a changing table, set up a blanket/pad on a solid surface or the floor and lay the baby on her back.

- Unlatch the stickies holding the baby's diaper on.

- While gently holding the baby's ankles together, lift up her legs and wipe the bottom with clean wipes or a wet, warm rag. For a little boy, you may want to place another wet rag or wipe over the penis so you do not get sprayed.

- Wipe a girl from front to back. Be sure to get all the excrement off the baby's skin.

- While you are still holding the baby's legs up, pull out the diaper in a downward motion and roll it up into a ball. Throw it into the trash or disposal container if you can do so without letting go of the baby.

- If the parents want you to put powder, lotion or ointment on the baby, put it on now.

- Finally, slide a clean diaper under baby's bottom and place her legs back down over the elastic leg spots on the sides of the diaper. Pull up the top half over the baby's belly and attach the stickies on either side of the baby's hips. If you are changing a boy, be sure his penis is not pointed up.

- When you're done, don't forget to wash your hands.

RHYTHMIC SOUNDS

Newborns are used to hearing the sounds in their mother's womb—the rhythmic *thump thump thump* of her heart and the *woosh woosh* of the fluids in her body. It's not quiet in there! Sometimes the creaking of a rocking chair, ticking of a clock, or even repeating "shhh, shhh, shhh" or "wooosh, wooosh, wooosh" in a rhythm can help to calm down a baby. Try a classical music or ocean sounds CD. These are great things to bring with you when you babysit.

TENDER TOUCH

To calm down a baby who is upset, angry, or scared, it is helpful to touch and hold her. Did you ever wonder why hugs and massages are so relaxing? Human touch causes the release of special chemicals in the baby's brain that help to relax and calm her. Hold her hand or stroke her head and cuddle that little one close to you.

SUCKING

The sucking reflex is strong in new babies. Often they try to root and may look hungry without wanting to eat. They might just want to suck! If it's okay with the parents, give the baby a pacifier to suck when she seems anxious, agitated, or nervous. It's also good to suck after eating and while sleeping, which helps to reduce the risk of SIDS (Sudden Infant Death Syndrome). If the parents do not want you to give the baby a pacifier, she can suck on her hand or another toy, but make sure it is clean!

SWADDLING

Babies are used to a small, tight, cozy space. Out in the big wide world it is not only cooler and brighter, there is also nothing to constrict movement. This can be a bit overwhelming and frightening to a baby who puts out her arm and just hits air and more air. New babies feel more secure when they are swaddled. This means wrapping them up in a blanket a special way. The tight wrap helps to control their startle reflex as well. You might notice an infant's arms flail out when her head bends back or if something in the room scares her. This flail reflex typically disappears around two to three months of age, but in some babies it can occur up to four months, so don't be surprised if you notice it in a baby you are watching.

Swaddling not only helps with startling, it also keeps a baby warm, at a temperature she is more comfortable with. Be sure that the baby is not too warm, since she cannot regulate her own body temperature. She should only be wearing very light clothing or just a diaper, and don't swaddle if the room is too warm.

Make sure you ease the transition from one activity to another and avoid over-stimulating the baby with too many sounds, sights, or smells. She is so little, it is easy for her to become overwhelmed!

How to Swaddle

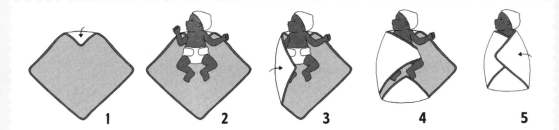

→ Get a baby blanket that is made from cotton or a similar material that won't easily stretch out.

→ Place the blanket on a firm, safe surface with the top corner pointing up, like a diamond. Fold that top corner down.

→ Next, put the baby on his back on to the blanket. That top fold should be right under his little neck.

→ It should now look like the baby is lying on a diamond with no top point. There will be a point by his right arm, a point by his left, and a bottom point under his feet.

→ Take the corner that's near the baby's right arm and pull it across his body.

→ Tuck that corner under his left arm and around under his back.

→ Now take the bottom point. Pull it up over his tummy and gently tuck it under the right side of the baby's neck and head.

→ Now you have one more point left, near the baby's left arm. Take the last point and pull it across his body to the right. Tuck it under his back on his right side. If you have enough blanket, pull it across his back and over to his left side.

→ Hold the little bundle close and rock him gently, while singing, talking, or making shushing sounds.

If a baby is over eight weeks old, make sure it is okay with the parents to try swaddling. For older babies, it's better to keep the legs loose in the wrap.

Toddlers

Between twelve and twenty-four months (one to two years) toddlers often have problems controlling their feelings and emotions. They tend to over-express things and become very dramatic. That's totally normal for this age.

Toddlers often have comfort objects like a teddy bear, doll, or blanket. When they are crying or upset, bring them this special object and ask the child to give it a hug. These special objects can help them self-soothe and self-calm when upset.

Music can also help a toddler forget he is angry. Find a CD or radio station that you can dance to. Play the music in the background and ask the child if he wants to dance. If you get an angry or pouty "no," start to dance yourself. This works especially well if the child has a favorite song or CD.

It's okay to be silly! Sometimes a sad child needs a laugh more than she knows. Act like a clown for her! Put a stuffed animal on your head or make funny faces. Bringing the child into the action can help as well. Give her a stuffed animal to put on her own head and ask if she can balance it up there. Funny things distract the child from tears or sad thoughts.

Preschool-Aged Kids

By this age, children are old enough to understand why they are angry or sad and can clearly express it. They are also more conversational. Here are some good ways to get the child talking about why she is upset (or to comfort her if she doesn't want to talk):

- Ask the child why she is sad and try to talk about her feelings.
- Take out some paper and crayons. Ask her to draw a picture about how she is feeling.
- Take out some dolls or action figures. Ask if the child would like to tell her dolls about the angry or sad feelings. You can even begin a make-believe play with the dolls to help the child express her feelings. Use the dolls to repeat what happened in real life. Start the scenario yourself

and see if the child picks up playing with you. Playing make-believe is a fantastic way for a child to work out anger, especially when she does not feel like talking or has problems saying what she feels.

Ask if the child wants a hug.

Ask if the child would like to hug her favorite doll or toy.

Change the subject and introduce something fun to do, like "Hey! Want to go outside and play on your swing set?" or "Meghan, can you show me how this bomerangadoozle works?"

Remember, don't yell at an angry child—raising your voice only makes the child raise her own voice in competition.

School-Age Kids

Comforting an older child generally involves discussion. Talk to her about what's making her sad and what she wants to do. Let her know that she doesn't have to talk, but you are there to listen if she wants to. Talk about your own experiences when you were younger and had a babysitter, or what you remember from your own life about the situation that is upsetting her. Personal experiences and reflections can help you reach out to her. You can also try giving her some alone time in her room to write or draw.

And remember, even older kids need a hug sometimes!

CHAPTER 6
Fighting

Dealing with a Feud

Children will fight with each other—it's a fact of life. Often you'll run into a spell of anger when you're babysitting. It's important to address this in the correct way. Remember to discuss discipline with the parents. As with the rest of your time babysitting, it's essential to set limits, be consistent, and mirror healthy behavior.

When children get angry or become fussy and you can't figure out why, remember that they may be tired, bored, or hungry. Try to talk out the problem to figure out why they are upset. If that doesn't work, here are some useful tips to make the fighting stop:

Toddlers

When a toddler is in a bad mood or throws a temper tantrum, he could be making a statement that he *needs your acknowledgment*. Sharing simple exercises to build a relationship with the child you are babysitting for is a good step in positive care. Activities such as reading together, making dinner together, and pointing out different objects on a walk around the block are simple but effective bonding and learning experiences that help to minimize anxiety, stress, and anger in young children. Believe it or not, stress affects even little kids, and can make a huge difference in their attitudes and how quick they are to argue. Relaxing activities, talking, and sharing help ease the stress that can lead to anger and fighting, and can help prevent a lot of arguments before they happen. If the children start fighting, try introducing a relaxing activity. It can really help calm down the situation!

Remember to keep communication open. Allow a child to complete what he is saying, uninterrupted. Have patience. Understanding a child is fundamental for his healthy development.

Allow children to make mistakes, but set limits, be consistent, and express the behavior you want the child to learn. Be willing to say no and stick to it.

Preschoolers

At this age, arguments and tantrums may come from a variety of situations. Preschool children often get angry over sharing toys—especially around babysitters who may act differently than parents. With two or three children, toys become prizes, and friends or siblings will fight over something that may seem interesting one moment and boring the next.

Speak to the child who had the toy first. Set a time limit for play and encourage sharing after that time limit. "You can play with this for fifteen minutes, and then Abby gets a turn for fifteen minutes." Allow the child to pass on the toy after the limit is up. If he or she does not obey, take the toy away.

Find another toy in the meantime to replace the desire for the one the child wants. Pick out something in the room that looks fascinating and make a big deal about it. "Wow, Abby, look at this pony! While Kayla has the castle, you can play with this pretty pony with the rainbow hair." Encourage the child to play, and you can even play along to make it more interesting! "Look, I can brush her hair. Wow—it gets so shiny when you brush it. Do you want to try?" Be careful, though. You don't want to make the new toy so fabulous that the children begin fighting over that one instead.

If this doesn't work, you may find that the best solution is to take away the item from both kids. This especially works with the younger ones, such as four- and five-year-olds fighting over a toy truck. Let them both pick out another toy and put the truck in a place where they can see it but not reach it, such as on top of the refrigerator. This way if they start to fight over another toy, you can look up at the truck with a look that warns them that if they don't stop fighting, their other toys could end up on top of the fridge.

School-Aged Kids

Older kids know the rules. Start by letting them know that. Generally, fighting is born from an activity that is not allowed, such as hitting. Tell the children they will have to stop playing with their friends if they don't stop their misbehavior, for example "Sam will have to go home if you don't stop hitting your sister."

You can also try the guilt tactic with older children. "Kylie, you've been so good all day, what's going on now? Are you not feeling well?" If you act surprised and disappointed by their bad behavior, older children will often stop fighting so as not to disappoint you or their parents.

Just as with younger kids, introducing a new activity can sometime distract the kids from fighting and focus them on something else in a positive way. Think of something you can do that will take their attention in a whole new direction, such as going for a walk, watching a movie, or starting a crafts project. If they were already doing an activity, stop that activity until they are done fighting.

Remember to ask the parents if they have special "fighting rules" for their children.

Sibling Rivalry

With sibling rivalry, you can often think of funny games to help the siblings bond. When a little tension arises, try pulling out a mirror and making them both stare at each other in it. Kids will often make silly faces and eventually end up laughing at each other and at themselves, forgetting whatever started their silly argument in the first place.

Remember that it's not always the older child's fault. Don't be quick to judge or blame. If you didn't see the incident that started the fighting, listen to both sides of the story, and then choose new activities for both children.

If it gets violent, be sure to separate fighting kids! You don't want anyone to get hurt. They'll probably tell you "He started it!" Tell them that it doesn't matter who "started" the fighting—they're both arguing and both need to be separated until they calm down and cool off. Try moving the fighting kids to different areas to play with different toys.

A child will often feel or say that his brother or sister is not as good as him. When this happens it is important to sit both children down and focus on the good things each child possesses. Ask both of them to name three things that are good about themselves, and then three things that are good about their sibling. You can even make it into an art project— write the special qualities on construction paper or draw pictures to illustrate those qualities.

Temper Tantrums

There are many reasons that a child will turn from a sweet, happy, bouncy angel to a screaming little terror, and there's usually no way to predict it. Don't blame yourself or even the parents—it happens. A child may throw a tantrum if you tell him he cannot have a cookie until after dinner when he insists he wants it "NOW!!!!!" Or maybe you decide it's too cold to go outside without a coat and the child simply *will not* wear one. Remember to stay calm. You're the big person, he's the little person. Take a deep breath and let it out slowly. Speak in a calm voice. Yelling will only aggravate the situation even more when the child follows your lead and starts yelling back. The other magical thing about speaking quietly is that even though the child is throwing a fit, he probably wants to know what you're saying, so he'll have to be quiet to hear you, if only for a moment. That moment can stop the escalation of a tantrum.

Generally, you'll find kids two to five years old going through these little fits, often whining, kicking, and screaming. When children get older, you can reason with them a little better and explain why the rule has been set. With an older child you can even talk about why he's angry and ask for his suggestions in the situation. Unfortunately, younger kids are the ones who usually throw the tantrums, and they don't always think or care about WHY…they just want it their way.

So what are they throwing a tantrum about? Think about something they might want or something they want to do and focus on it. You can turn an angry situation into a happy one. For example, "You *can* play on the jungle gym if we go outside, but you have to wear your coat to play on the jungle gym." Or "You *can* have the candy after dinner, but you must eat a healthy dinner before you can have the candy." Mention what they want several times in the sentence so they know you are addressing the situation. Not only will this get their attention, it will show them you really do care about the things that matter to them. Just be sure you follow through with your promise!

If a child still won't listen to you, it might help for you to start playing with something they love to do. For example, take out the crayons, sit down at the table, and start coloring. You don't even have to ask the child to join you. As a matter of fact, it often works better if you don't. The child will probably come up to you to see what you're doing and want to join you. Be nice, even if the child was mean to you. Children speak what's on their mind and don't mean to hurt with what they say. They may hate you one second and love you the next. Things said in a temper tantrum may be hateful, but remember not to take it personally.

Punishment

Preschool, elementary, and middle school children have the ability to know right from wrong. Babies do not. Do not try to punish a baby for doing something you may consider "wrong" or "bad." A baby will not understand. It is okay to teach him what he cannot do, but do not punish him for doing it. For example, if a six-month-old is pulling on a cord in the living room, take it away from him and tell him "No," or "You will get hurt," and hide the cord so he can't get to it again. Then redirect his activity to something else. He probably just thinks it's a toy, so give him a toy he *can* play with.

Discuss with the parents what their form of punishment is for their child or children. Be specific about a child doing something wrong—what should you do? Remember, punishment isn't pointless cruelty to a child who did something wrong; it should be part of learning and growing. For something to be acknowledged as punishment by the child so it will decrease the chance of the behavior occurring again, it must happen immediately after bad behavior occurs. The closer to the behavior the punishment occurs, the greater its effect will be. It is important to understand the history behind the situation. Has a child been punished often? Is that punishment just an annoyance or something he truly dislikes? The more intense the punishment is, the greater the chance a child's bad behavior will decrease. But remember, you should follow the parents' rules for punishment. Don't make up your own.

CHAPTER 7
Activities and Crafts

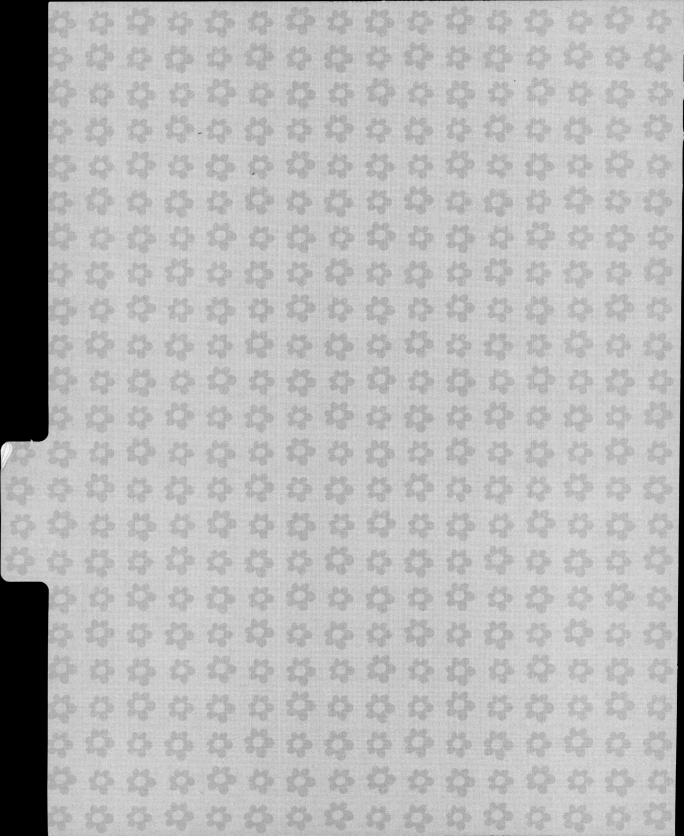

Have Fun!

When babysitting little ones, remember not to give small, solid foods such as hard candies, nuts, and popcorn to children under the age of three. Foods like grapes, mini tomatoes, and hot dogs should be smooshed or diced into very small pieces. These foods can get lodged in young children's throats and cause choking. Infants put everything in their mouths! Wash toys if they become dirty and be sure they cannot be swallowed. As a general rule, if it is small enough to fit in a toilet paper roll, it's too small for a child under three. Keep such toys away from babies and look for something safer to play with. Some easy activities include arts and crafts, backyard play, reading, going for a walk, and playing make-believe. Parents will be happy that their kids are involved with activities that will help them learn and grow, and kids will be thrilled to try new games!

As you're planning your activities, remember, do not let young children play with anything that has a cord, long string, or sharp ends, like the string hanging from the mini-blinds or that barbecue fork in the kitchen drawer. If you have a battery-operated toy, do not put it in the bathtub or kiddy pool (unless it is designed to go there and has been manufactured for water safety). As a general rule, don't get anything wet that is not a bath toy, unless it has been pointed out by the parents as okay to use.

Is It Okay to Play with Make-believe Guns?

Ask parents if they allow their children to play with make-believe guns. Lots of boys like to pretend they're cowboys or police officers, so this may come up. If it's okay with parents, be sure that the child is playing with a make-believe gun in a safe manner. Both toys and imaginary guns should be pointed away from people at all times. The make-believe play should be centered on a safe, nonviolent, gun-toting person, like a cowboy shooting at a target or a space hero shooting at an alien to protect the ship.

If the children are not allowed to use guns and you see one of them using a hand or another toy as a gun, redirect the activity. Pretend it is a fire hose and say "Wow! Keep shooting that water on the fire. It's doing a great job to put it out!" Or maybe it's a flashlight and you can say "Melissa! That's great! Aim that flashlight in the woods over by that chair so Becky can find her way home!" Use your imagination to change the focus of their game.

Chapter four contained a list of age-appropriate activities. Below are more activities and crafts for kids of all ages. As you come up with additional ideas or hear about something that the kids enjoy, write them down and keep them handy.

ANIMAL HUNT

Bring a notebook on a walk or into the backyard and have the children write down or draw every different species they see. If you want, you can make the hunt more specific and just look for a certain kind of creature, like bugs or birds.

NAME THAT TUNE

Play just a tiny bit of a song and ask the child to guess what song it is. Be sure to use songs the children will be familiar with.

PLAY CARDS

Get a pack of cards and play a game like Go Fish or War. If you're feeling ambitious, you could even make up your own card game.

SCAVENGER HUNT

Make a list of silly things the children have to find and check off or put a gold star sticker on the paper every time they find one. This could be indoors *(Find a blond-haired doll or a green block)* or outdoors *(Find a pinecone or a gray pebble).* If you are babysitting more than one child, it might be fun for them to create their own scavenger hunt lists and then swap.

MUSICAL OBJECTS

Set out things to sit on in a wide-open space, like outdoors or the play-room. These can be a baby blanket, a coloring book, etc. Play this just like musical chairs. You play music, and when the music stops, yell out the name of one item on the floor. The child must quickly find and sit on that object. If he doesn't find it, take it away, until all the items are gone.

Arts and Crafts

Kids of all ages love arts and crafts. Children will usually have their own craft supplies, but if you're unsure about what they have or if you have a specific project in mind, you may want to create a babysitting bag full of your own supplies. This not only allows you to control what the kids play with, but parents will be impressed that you're so prepared.

Here are some ideas about what to put into your babysitting bag:

construction paper

kid-safe glue

glitter

crayons

watercolor paint

feathers, buttons, and other things to
   glue onto paper (for kids over three)

fingerpaint

old shirts for smocks

kid-safe scissors (with rounded tips)

chalk

toilet paper tubes

old sponges that are clean and dry

empty egg cartons

pipe cleaners

a handful of cereal pieces, such as
   toasted O's or corn puff balls

small pieces of cut felt or material

kid-safe paint

Use your imagination. All sorts of weird objects can become craft supplies. Kids will know what to do with them, so lay out the materials and let them get to work. Below are some great art projects in case the kids need direction. If the kids are too young to do these projects on their own, you will need to help them, especially with cutting. Always put down newspaper in the work area for easy cleanup.

FISH

Get a paper plate and cut a wedge out of the left side—like a pizza slice. Glue or tape the wedge, point in, on the right side as a tail. The space you cut out is the mouth of the fish. Draw an eye on the fish and let the child decorate it with crayons or markers, drawing fins and scales. You can even punch a hole in the top and hang it!

HANDPRINT FLOWERS

Put a little bit of kid-safe paint on a paper plate. If the child isn't old enough to do so alone, place her hand in the paint and cover her palm with paint. Lift up the little hand and help the child press it down onto a piece of construction paper (toward the top of the paper). Repeat this step three or four times in a row so that the top of the paper is covered in palm prints. While the paint is drying, have the child wash her hands. When the paper is dry, allow the child to draw stems and leaves below the hands as if the hands were flowers.

VEGGIE PRINTS

Ask the parents if you can use a squash, apple, potato, or other firm piece of food for an art project. Put a little bit of kid-safe paint on a paper plate. Cut the veggie in half or thirds, making a good size to hold in your hand. Have the child dip the flat side of the vegetable into the paint, then press it onto a piece of construction paper to make a print, like a stamp. Make as many prints as you want on the sheet of paper. If you have a long roll of white paper, or even a paper bag, this is a fun way to make your own wrapping paper.

WHIPPED CREAM PAINTING

Squirt a little bit of whipped cream onto a paper plate. Put one drop of food coloring on the cream and allow the child to squish it up with her hands. Have paper ready so she can make a design, handprint, or squiggles with her fingers.

INSTRUMENTS

Get some empty bottles of different sizes. You may want to ask the parents if they have a plastic water or soda bottle in the recycling bin. Peel off the labels and clean the bottles out. While they are drying, collect a bunch of little noise-making items, such as macaroni noodles, buttons, or rice. You won't need more than a handful. Help the child drop the items into the bottles. Screw the lid back on and allow the child to color on the side of the bottles with crayons. When you're done, turn on some music and shake them to the beat!

TOUCH AND FEEL BOOK

One fun activity is creating a touch-and-feel book. You will need a variety of different textured materials such as cotton balls, scraps of velvet fabric, aluminum foil, sandpaper, or dried leaves. You'll also need construction paper, crayons, scissors, and a stapler to make the book. Set out paper and help the child glue different textures onto different pages. Let the pages dry and then staple them together. Write a descriptive word such as "rough," "smooth," or "shiny" on each page and encourage the child to feel the objects and talk about what she notices.

When you're done, add a blank sheet on the cover. If the child can write her name, write "_____'s Book" and have her fill it in. If she is too young, hold her hand and write the letters with her.

MY NAME

Write the child's name in big block or bubble letters on a sheet of paper. For each letter, let the child choose something she likes or an activity she likes to do, then use crayons or markers to color in and design the letter based upon the activity she chooses. For example, KYLIE: K = Kites, Y = Yellow, L = Lions, I = Ice Cream E = Elephants.

Drawing with Children

Toddlers and preschool kids often draw pictures that seem very clear and obvious to them, but that look like a scribble or a bunch of lines to an adult. It can hurt their feelings if they show you a picture of a squiggle that they are proud of and you ask them what it is. Instead, ask them to tell you about the picture. This will allow them to explain what it is without being insulted that you couldn't identify the squiggly line as their best friend or their pet.

LETTER HOLDER

Get two paper plates and cut one in half. Staple the plates together. The half plate will become a pouch to put notes or letters in. Staple or tape a string across the top of the whole plate so the child can hang the letter holder on a doorknob. Write "My Notes" in big letters across the pouch and have her decorate the holder with crayons, markers, stickers, or stamps. When the letter holder is done, the child's siblings or parents can leave notes in it for her—just like her own mailbox.

SOCK PUPPETS

Get a few old socks, stickers, and markers. Put a sock over your hand. When you open and close your hand, you can turn it into a puppet! The thumb is the bottom of the mouth and the four fingers are the top. Put stickers on the head for features like the eyes, nose and mouth. You can even make silly animals; draw whiskers to make a cat or a big round nose for a pig. Once you have made a few, have a puppet show or play a make-believe game with your puppets. Unless you've brought your own socks, be sure to ask the parents before you draw anything on the socks.

WHAT'S THAT CLOUD?

You know how you can look up in the clouds and use your imagination to find pictures and objects? Well you can do that on paper, too! Take a crayon, marker, or pen and draw a bunch of twisted, twirly, loopy, scribbly lines on a sheet of paper. Then sit with the child you are babysitting and see if the two of you can find things together! You can even use other colors to pick out, color in, or expand upon the shapes you find!

PUZZLES

Find an old magazine, a pencil, glue or a glue stick, scissors, and a piece of cardboard. Have the child pick out a picture and glue it onto the cardboard. Then let her draw (or help her draw) odd-shaped lines like puzzle pieces across the picture with a pencil. Be sure you don't put too many lines because you will want fairly large pieces. Cut or have the child cut on the lines to make the pieces separate. Mix them up and have the child put them together again like a puzzle!

Seasonal crafts are fun to make, too. Here are some fun and easy projects:

AUTUMN LEAVES

Go on a leaf hunt in the backyard! Pick up different colored leaves and glue them onto construction paper. You can even let the child color and glitter the leaves. This is good for ages two and up, just watch that the little ones don't eat the leaves.

If you don't have any fallen leaves to pick up, you can make your own. Pick out red, brown, and yellow crayons. Tape the three crayons together to make one fat crayon, and then let the child scribble on a sheet of paper with the tri-colored crayon. This will make a wonderful mixture of fall colors. When she is done, fold the paper into quarters and cut out the shape of a leaf.

TURKEY HAND

Trace the child's hand onto a sheet of white paper and round off the bottom by drawing a line from the bottom of the thumb to the bottom of the pinkie. This is going to be a turkey! Under this line, draw two turkey legs. The child's thumb is the head. Put a little eye in the top and a squiggly red wattle under the chin. The four fingers are the turkey's feathers. Let the child color the turkey's head and body. Add a wing in the center. Pick out different colors for the feathers and color each finger-feather in.

WINTER SNOWFLAKES

Cut or help the child cut snowflake shapes out of coffee filters. After they are cut, help him glue them onto dark blue construction paper. The glue will squish through the holes as he spreads it with their fingers and can be sprinkled with clear and/ or silver glitter. The snowflakes make great holiday cards that kids can share with their friends. This project is good for Valentine's Day, too. Just use red paper and cut out hearts instead of snowflakes.

If snow doesn't fall in your part of the country, you can take this opportunity to talk to the child about snow.

REINDEER

Trace the child's foot onto a dark brown piece of construction paper and her hands onto a piece of light brown construction paper or a paper bag. Cut out the foot (this is the head) and hands (these are the antlers). Glue the antlers on the top of the head. Decorate with a big red nose, an eye, and a mouth.

SPRING FLOWERS

Put water in two or three glasses. In each glass, put one drop of food coloring. Fold a coffee filter in half, and then again in half, and hand it to the child. Let her dip a corner of the filter into each color. Place the wet filter on a plate or foil to dry. When it is dry, open the coffee filter. Pinch and twist the center of the filter. Attach a green pipe cleaner by wrapping the end of the pipe cleaner around the piece you have pinched, which should be sticking out.

PAPER BUGS

Let the child color a paper plate with crayons. From construction paper cut out circles that will be used for spots, two strips that will be used for antennae, and two oval shapes that will be used for wings. After the child colors the body, help him glue the body parts on.

SUMMER SEASHORE ART

(For this craft, you'll need to bring some sand.) Encourage the child to draw a picture of the beach on a piece of paper or a plate. When the drawing is complete, put glue over the sections of the picture that will have sand. Help the child shake sand onto the picture and then set it aside to dry. When the picture is dry, invite him to touch and feel the sand art!

SUMMERTIME MOBILE

Get a hanger, some yarn or string, construction paper, and magazines. Give the magazines to the child and let her find pictures that remind her of summertime, like a beach ball, a sun, or someone on a skateboard. Help the child cut out the pictures and glue them onto the construction paper. Then cut around each picture, leaving a small border of paper. Punch a hole in the top of each one and tie a six inch piece of string through each hole. Tie the pictures onto the hanger by their strings. On a nice, breezy day, you can take the mobile outside and see how the wind blows the summer objects around.

If you prefer projects that don't use the typical arts-and-crafts supplies, try some of the activities listed below.

PLAY-DOUGH

(Before you begin this activity, ask for permission to "cook" in the kitchen. It's a good idea to show the parents what you plan to make before you begin. Remember, keep the kids AWAY from the stove.)
YOU NEED: 1 cup flour, ½ cup salt, 1 package unsweetened powdered drink mix, 1 tbsp oil, 1 cup boiling water
DIRECTIONS: Mix the flour, salt, and drink mix together. Add the oil and the boiling water. Stir the mixture until it is well blended. Remove the mixture from the bowl and knead it until it forms a soft dough that you can play with. Then let the kids build all kinds of fun objects with the dough.

GELATIN SHAPES

(Before you begin this activity, ask for permission to "cook" in the kitchen. It's a good idea to show the parents what you plan to make before you begin. Remember, keep the kids AWAY from the stove.)

YOU NEED: 3 envelopes unflavored gelatin, ¾ cup boiling water, 1 12-oz. can each of frozen apple, orange, grape, or other juice concentrate

DIRECTIONS: This is a good one to start when you first get to the house so it will have time to settle. Dissolve the gelatin in boiling water, and then separate it into 3 different bowls, one for each juice flavor. Add one different can of juice to each different bowl of gelatin and stir until mixed. When you add the frozen juice to the bowl of gelatin it will melt quickly since the water will still be warm. Stir it up until it's completely melted. This is something the kids can help with.

Next, pour the gelatin-juice mixture into 3 lightly greased pans (one for each juice flavor) and chill in the refrigerator for several hours. When the gelatin is firm, give the kids cookie cutters and let them cut out shapes. They'll have fun playing with their food, and will enjoy sampling the different tastes.

PEANUT BUTTER PLAY-DOUGH

YOU NEED: 2 cups peanut butter, 2 cups powdered milk, 1 cup honey or corn syrup

DIRECTIONS: Mix all of the ingredients together in a bowl. Then give the child a cookie sheet or plastic tray, and a small ball of dough. Let him smoosh and mold it, and try a little nibble! It's fun to create shapes with and it's delicious!

WRAP IT UP

YOU NEED: ½ cup water, 1 tsp dishwashing soap, food coloring, a plastic cup, a baking sheet, a plastic drinking straw, white drawing paper, and markers

DIRECTIONS: Mix water, soap, and a few drops of food coloring in a plastic cup, and then place the plastic cup on a baking sheet. Put the straw in the cup and blow bubbles through the straw until they spill all over the baking sheet. Remove the cup and place a piece of paper on top of the bubbles. Lift the paper off gently. The colored bubbles will create a light design on the paper.

Let it dry and then the child can draw on it.

This is a fun project for making stationery or book covers, but make sure the kids are only blowing out through the straw so that they do not swallow any soap.

BUBBLE TIME

YOU NEED: 1 cup water, ⅓ cup dish soap, 2 tablespoons light corn syrup

DIRECTIONS: Mix all of the ingredients together in a large bowl. Then use a stretched-open wire hanger to make a bubble wand that you can blow through or swoosh through the air. You can also use the child's beach or bath toys to make bubbles. Look for a plastic toy that has a hole in it. Dip the toy into the bowl, covering the hole completely with the bubble liquid, then lift the toy out and gently swing it or blow into it to make bubbles!

SOLID OR LIQUID?

YOU NEED: 1½ cups water, food coloring, 2 cups cornstarch, wax paper

DIRECTIONS: In a large bowl, slowly mix the water and a few drops of food coloring into the cornstarch. When it is mixed, let the kids play with this weird substance over a sheet of wax paper. Is it solid or liquid? Actually, it's both at the same time!

SAND JARS

YOU NEED: sand, food coloring, clear sealable jars, plastic cups

DIRECTIONS: Pour sand into a few plastic cups and let the kids mix in food coloring to add color to the sand (you may want to add a little water to help disperse the color). When the sand is dry, pour it into a clear jar (an old tomato sauce jar works well), layering the colors any way they want. When the jar is full, put on the lid and let the kids display their art in their room.

CHAPTER 8
Time to Eat

Yummy!

As the babysitter, you will likely have to feed the children at some point. Before you start to cook anything, make sure you know whether the child has any food allergies that you should look out for.

Most kids can eat on their own, but babies are another story. If you have to feed a baby, first find out if the baby is on a schedule or eats on demand. Follow the schedule closely, or in the case of demand feeding (many breastfeeding babies are on-demand), be sure to have a bottle ready for when the baby gets fussy. Ask the parents when the best time is to try to feed him.

Remember to WASH YOUR HANDS before handling the bottle.

Find out how the parents want you to warm the bottles. They might have an appliance called a bottle warmer that heats up the milk or formula. Typically, heating a pot of water to a simmer and then placing the sealed bottle of milk or formula in the pot is the best way to warm a bottle. Microwaves can heat unevenly, overcook formula and breast milk, and kill important nutrients.

To check the temperature of the bottle, shake it to distribute the heat evenly and then squirt a bit of milk onto the inside of your wrist or the inside of your elbow (you may need to squeeze the nipple a bit). These are the most sensitive parts of your body and will be the best judge of the temperature. If it feels cool on your skin, place it back in the hot water or bottle warmer for a few minutes and check it again. If it stings your skin, the bottle is too warm. Put it in the refrigerator for a few minutes then check it again. It should never feel hot on your skin. You want it to feel lukewarm and comfortable.

When you are ready to feed the baby, hold her securely in your lap with one

arm around her and her head resting by your elbow. The rooting reflex is important in getting a baby to eat. This reflex is an automatic reaction newborn babies have; if something lightly brushes their cheeks, it makes them turn their heads and start sucking. To start the feeding, brush a finger across the baby's cheek closest to your body. The baby should turn her face toward you and her lips should part slightly.

Gently push the nipple of the bottle into the baby's open mouth, keeping her head and upper body raised at a slight angle so that it's easier for the baby to swallow. Tip the end of the bottle up as you're feeding so that the baby doesn't swallow air with breast milk or formula.

Once you have finished feeding the baby, remember to burp her. Babies will take in some air while drinking a bottle and burping helps to get rid of this air so they don't have gas or tummy cramps.

Use soft, gentle pats on the baby's back. You can hold the baby over your shoulder or across your legs with her tummy on your lap. Remember that the baby might spit up, so keep a burp cloth handy or place one under her chin.

Older kids may be easier to feed, but they tend to be picky. If this happens, try to remind them that snacks and mealtime can be fun, especially when you prepare the food together. Starting on page 74 there is a list of fun recipes you can try out. Before you make any of these, be sure to get the parents' permission to use the stove. As you find more recipes, write them down and keep them somewhere you can easily find them.

Sanitation

Anytime you are working with food, remember to wash your hands. The children should wash their hands, too. In order to make sure their hands are fully clean, the child should wash for 20 seconds. Try singing "The Alphabet Song," "Twinkle Twinkle Little Star," or "Mary Had a Little Lamb" to time the hand-washing process.

If you are working with anything uncooked—such as chicken breasts—be sure to wipe all surfaces with a sanitized wipe or soap and warm water. Do not let anything that touched the uncooked food (such as a spoon) touch anything else. If it does, put it in the sink and wash it.

Stove Safety

Keep handles of pots and pans turned away from the front of the stove so they don't stick out over the edge and cannot be grabbed by little hands and knocked over.

Don't let the children near the oven as you are putting food in, or taking it out. Make sure they are not behind you where you can trip over them with a hot pan in your hand.

Breakfast (you don't have to eat breakfast only in the morning)

FRUIT CREPE

YOU NEED: 2 eggs, 1 tablespoon milk or cream, a dash of salt, 1 tablespoon oil, plain or vanilla yogurt, about ½ cup fruit (cut up strawberries, bananas, peaches, blueberries, etc.), 1 tablespoon brown sugar

DIRECTIONS: Mix the eggs with the milk and salt, and beat with a fork for a few minutes. The child can do this while you heat the oil in a pan on low to medium heat. When the oil starts to sizzle, pour the egg mixture in the pan and cook until the edges are light brown. With a spatula, gently flip over. Keep the kids away from the stove for this in case there is a hot splatter of oil. Once the other side is lightly browned, remove it from the pan and place it on a plate. Let the child spoon some yogurt and fruit on top. Sprinkle with brown sugar and enjoy!

HOLY EGG!

(This recipe is for two, but you can make as many as you need.)

YOU NEED: a small drinking glass or round cookie cutter, 2 slices of bread, butter, 2 eggs, 2 slices of American cheese

DIRECTIONS: With the cookie cutter or drinking glass, cut out a hole in the center of each bread slice. You can help the child with this part. Spread butter the pan and put the bread on it. Put the pan over low heat. Next, open one egg and drop it into the hole in the slice of bread. Repeat for the second slice. Cook the egg until it's no longer jiggly for sunny side up. You can flip the egg and bread over for a more fully cooked egg. Once the egg is cooked, put a slice of cheese on the top of the bread. Allow it to melt for a few moments. Then take the slices off the pan with a spatula and serve when cool.

Lunch

HAPPY SALADS

YOU NEED: cottage cheese, 1 can of round pineapple slices, toppings (raisins, nuts, trail mix, shredded carrots, bean sprouts, etc.)

DIRECTIONS: Put some cottage cheese in a bowl for each serving. Spread it flat with the back of a spoon. Put one slice of pineapple on top of the cottage cheese; this is the face. Allow the child to use the toppings to design the face. Raisins make great eyes, and shredded carrots and bean sprouts make great hair!

MINI PIZZAS

YOU NEED: 2 or 3 English muffins, spaghetti sauce, shredded cheese, pepperoni

DIRECTIONS: Together, split open the English muffins and place them faceup on a plate. Next, spoon some sauce over the bread until each slice is covered. Take a handful of cheese and sprinkle it over the sauce. Finish with a few slices of pepperoni. Stick them in the toaster oven on the bake setting until the cheese starts to bubble.

SNAKE SALAD

YOU NEED: cucumber, zucchini, carrots, cream cheese

DIRECTIONS: Carefully slice up the veggies. Spread cream cheese on one side of each slice and stick them together, stacking alternating slices of each vegetable to make a colorful snake.

PIGGIES IN A SLEEPING BAG

YOU NEED: hot dogs or small sausages, refrigerated dough, ketchup, mustard

DIRECTIONS: Preheat the oven to 450° degrees. Cut the hot dogs in half. If you are using sausage, brown it in a pan first. Flatten the dough and cut it into strips. Wrap each piece of meat in a strip of dough. Put the wraps on a cookie sheet and bake for ten minutes. On a plate, squirt some ketchup and mustard for dipping and serve with the piggies.

Dinner

PIZZA BURGERS

YOU NEED: 1 pound of ground beef, 1 cup melting cheese (cut into cubes), 1 can of tomato soup, 8 rolls or hamburger buns

DIRECTIONS: Cook the ground beef in a skillet over the stove until it is browned. Add the cheese and tomato soup to the skillet. Stir slowly until the cheese is melted and the ingredients are mixed.

Remove from heat and allow it to cool. Spoon the mixture onto the rolls and let the kids enjoy!

CHEESEDOG CHOWDA

YOU NEED: 4 hot dogs, 2 cans of potato soup, 1 cup milk, 1 can of corn, 1 cup shredded cheese

DIRECTIONS: Cut hot dogs into small pieces. Pour soup and milk into a saucepan and cook slowly over low heat. As you are stirring, add corn and hot dog pieces. Let simmer for about 10 minutes. Remove from heat, add cheese, stir, and serve when cooled.

SOUTHWEST SLOPPY JOES

YOU NEED: 1 pound of ground beef, 1 can of beans, 1 cup salsa, salt and pepper, hamburger buns

DIRECTIONS: Cook the ground beef in a skillet on top of the stove until it is browned. Once it's cooked, add the beans and stir over a low heat. Next, add the salsa and keep stirring. Season with salt and pepper and remove from heat. Allow to cool and spoon onto the rolls. Be ready with lots of napkins!

ITALIAN VILLA PASTA BOWL

YOU NEED: pasta (macaroni, spirals, or ziti work best), can of tomatoes (chopped works best, but you can also use pureed), pepperoni slices, dash of salt, pinch of basil, green bell pepper, shredded mozzarella, bread for dipping

DIRECTIONS: Boil water, cook pasta, and drain pasta. Put pasta back in the pot over low heat and add can of tomatoes. While stirring, add pepperoni, salt, and basil. Chop up pepper and add to the pasta. Add cheese and remove from heat. Serve in a bowl with some bread on the side for dipping.

Snacks

BANANA POPS

YOU NEED: sprinkles, diced nut topping, shredded coconut, mini marshmallows, chocolate chips, bananas, wooden sticks or skewers

DIRECTIONS: Sprinkle a few teaspoons of each topping on a plate. Put a handful of chocolate chips in a bowl and microwave for about one minute, or until they're soft. Stir the melted chocolate around in the bowl so it's smooth. Unpeel a banana and put a wooden stick through one end. Make sure the chocolate is still warm and soft, but not too hot, then have the child dip her banana into the chocolate. Next, help the child roll the chocolate-covered banana into the toppings. Place the finished pop on a plate and place in the freezer to cool.

SPIDERS

YOU NEED: creamy peanut butter, round crackers, thin stick pretzels, raisins

DIRECTIONS: Spread the peanut butter on the crackers and stick two together like a sandwich. Between the crackers, put four pretzel sticks on either side to make eight legs. On the top, put two little dollops of peanut butter for eyes, and then place raisins on the peanut butter.

SWEET BISCUITS

YOU NEED: toppings (nuts, raisins, dried cranberries, etc.), ½ cup butter, 1 table-spoon of cinnamon, 1 cup sugar, 1 or 2 packaged refrigerated biscuits,

DIRECTIONS: Preheat the oven to 350°. Grease or foil a pan. Sprinkle your toppings across the bottom of the pan (a good kid activity). Place the stick of butter in a microwave-safe cup and melt it about a minute, until it is liquid. Mix the sugar and cinnamon together. Show the child how to rip each biscuit into three or four pieces. Together roll the pieces in the bowl of cinnamon and sugar. Take the biscuit pieces and roll them into the toppings on the pan, covering the whole biscuit with the toppings. Set them up on the pan about one inch apart. Drizzle them with the melted butter.

Bake for 30–35 minutes. When they are done cooking, tilt the pan onto a plate so the biscuits roll off and cool. Once they are cooled, serve and enjoy!

HONEY MILK BALLS

YOU NEED: ½ cup honey or corn syrup, 1 cup dry milk solids (powdered milk), ½ cup peanut butter, ½ cup raisins

DIRECTIONS: Combine all ingredients in a bowl. Mix well, then knead by hand until blended. Shape into small balls. Makes about two dozen balls.

Make sure you have a container ready to store the leftovers. They don't need to be refrigerated, but using an airtight container or aluminum foil wrapped over a bowl will help to keep them soft.

MAPLE APPLE TREATS

YOU NEED: 2–3 apples, ¼ cup of cinnamon, ¼ cup of sugar, 1 cup of sour cream, 3 tablespoons of maple syrup, 10 graham crackers

DIRECTIONS: Cut the apples into slices and put them on a plate. Mix the cinnamon and sugar together. Let the child help sprinkle some of the cinnamon and sugar gently on the apples. In a bowl, mix the sour cream with the syrup and sprinkle with remaining cinnamon and sugar. Spoon the mixture onto the graham crackers and top with an apple slice.

BUGS ON A LOG

YOU NEED: "logs" made from any of these foods: celery stalks (cut to about 3 inches long), apples (cut in halves or quarters with cores removed), or carrot sticks (peeled and cut to about 3 inches long); make spreads using cream cheese, pineapple, cheese, pimento, peanut butter, or egg salad; "bugs," which can be raisins, Cheerios, fruit puffs, diced fruit pieces, or chocolate chips

DIRECTIONS: Top the logs with various spreads: cream cheese and pineapple, cheese and pimento, peanut butter, or egg salad. Then give the kids some "bugs" to put on the log: raisins, cheerios, fruit-puffs, diced fruit pieces, or chocolate chips.

SANDWICH SHAPES

YOU NEED: bread slices (white, wheat, rye, pumpernickel, etc.), cookie cutters, spreads (egg salad, peanut butter, or tuna fish)

DIRECTIONS: Let children cut out shapes from the bread slices with cookie cutters. Spread one of the healthy toppings over the bread and put the slices together to make a sandwich that is fun, delicious, and nutritious!

BAKE-LESS CAKE

YOU NEED: box of flat wafer cookies, whipped cream, fruit (berries, sliced apples, or bananas), chocolate syrup

DIRECTIONS: Start with a layer of wafer cookies on a plate. Spread cookies with whipped cream. Place a few pieces of fruit on the cream. Drizzle them with chocolate syrup. Then start another layer of cookies, another layer of cream, and another layer of fruit and chocolate syrup. Repeat a few times until the cake is as tall as you want it to be.

DRINK-A-FRUIT

YOU NEED: 1 cup of fresh or frozen berries, handful of ice cubes, 1 cup orange juice, 1 small yogurt (any flavor), 1 banana

DIRECTIONS: Make sure the blender is unplugged. Dump all ingredients into the blender one by one (kids can help dump them in as long as the blender pitcher is **not** connected to the power source). Once everything is inside and the cover is on the blender pitcher, plug in the blender and mix up the ingredients to make a chilly, yummy, drinkable fruit concoction!

CHAPTER 9
Bath Time

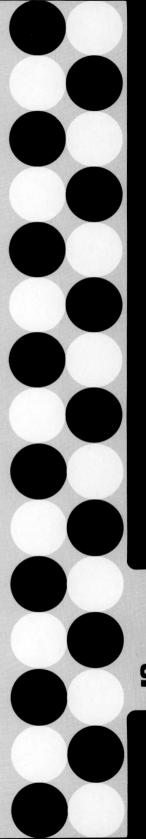

Scrub-a-Dub-Dub

One of the things parents may ask you to do is to give their child a bath before bedtime. This is often part of a nighttime routine that can help children go to sleep. Routines are important for children, and babies especially can be soothed by a warm bath before bed.

It's important to have all the things you need before going into the bathroom, that way you do not have to get up once the child is in the water. Lay a towel on the floor of the child's room and make yourself a bath kit. Bring the bath kit into the bathroom with the child. If anything on the list is already in the bathroom, be sure it is at arm's reach from the tub. If the parents have a cordless phone, take it into the bathroom with you as well.

Bathwater should be about 85–90 degrees. If you do not have a water thermometer, run the water to feel like a baby's bottle feels—warm, but not too hot. Check it with your elbow or the inside of your wrist.

Remember, NEVER leave a child alone in a bath. Kids can drown in just an inch of water.

Infants

A baby bath kit should include a clean diaper, fresh pajamas, several soft washcloths (you'll need one to soap up and wash the baby, a wet one without soap to rinse his face, a dry one to wipe his eyes if they get splashed with soap or water, and an extra one that may help entertain the baby if he tries to grab at the one you're using to wash him), and a towel. The parents may provide packaged baby bath cloths that have already been soaped up. In that case, just have a dry washcloth ready in case you need to wipe soap from his eyes. You will also need baby soap or "baby bath," baby shampoo, baby oil or lotion for after the bath (if the parents desire), and a blanket (babies are usually cold after getting out of the warm water).

The parents may also ask you to add something to the baby's bathwater, such as lavender wash for relaxation or eucalyptus for a cold. Be sure you know the exact amount to add, and don't put in more than the parents tell you to. Even extra bubble bath may make a baby sick, so stick to the correct amounts for babies.

For an infant, the parents may give you a small tub or special device that goes in the big tub. Be sure to ask the parents how to use it. If you're using the big tub, make sure you wait until the water is finished running and you have checked the temperature *before* you put a baby in the bath.

CLEANING: Babies generally have little rolls of fat, so be sure to clean under their neck, under their arms and legs, and behind their ears. Clean between the fingers and toes (this is a good time to play "This Little Piggy" or practice counting). Use gentle motions. Wipe the baby's face with a wrung-out washcloth that was wet with only water, not soap. For the diaper area, wipe front to back on baby girls, just like you would when changing their diapers.

Remember, babies get very slippery when they're wet, so keep a hand on the baby at all times!

HAVING FUN: Once the baby is clean, let her play in the water for a little while. Be sure it is still warm and that her little feet aren't getting too pruny, which is a sign that the baby has been in the bath too long. Pruny skin can also become uncomfortable and lead to dry skin. Have fun with the baby in the water! Show the little one how to pop bubbles, make her rubber ducky float, or squirt water at her from her toy fish. You can even sing bath-time songs to make it an enjoyable experience!

Toddlers

A toddler bath kit should include a clean diaper or pull-up (whichever the child will sleep in), fresh pajamas, several soft washcloths or packaged baby bath cloths if provided, a towel, child-friendly soap, child-friendly shampoo, a cup for hair washing, and any special bath toys the child requests (make sure you collect everything *before* you get into the bathroom).

A toddler can help clean herself in the bath, but you'll have to do most of the washing. Soap up two washcloths, one for you and one for the child. Guide her to each body part and gently scrub with the soapy cloth. This is also a great time to review body parts. "Where are your shoulders? Let's clean those shoulders! How about your knees?"

For a toddler's hair, you'll want to be prepared with a cup of warm water. Have the child lean back a bit and close her eyes. It helps to fold a warm dry washcloth over her eyes during this part. Then take the cup of warm water and pour it over her hair. Soap up her head (she may want to sit up during this part. Just be sure her hair is not too drippy or the soap will run into her eyes). Once the hair is shampooed, put the cloth back over her eyes, lean her back, and rinse out the toddler's hair with more warm water in a cup. Run warm water through the child's hair as often as necessary to get rid of all the soap. If the parents provide you with a spray faucet, you may not need the cup, but be careful you don't spray in the child's eyes or use too strong a stream. Always make sure the temperature of the water remains comfortable for the child.

For a toddler, bath time is more of an adventure than a cleaning experience. He or she may pretend to be a pirate or a mermaid. Toddlers usually have special toys or games they look forward to using in the water. Sometimes, though, toddlers will put up a fight about taking a bath. If that happens, try talking about *why* it is good to take a bath, how it helps us stay clean and healthy. You can also talk about creatures that go in the water, like dolphins, sharks, and goldfish, or what you can do in the water that you can't do on "dry land" such as squirting water, playing with floating toys, making bubbles, and splashing. Let the child pick out a water creature she wants to be and you can play make-believe in the bath. If you can make bath time sound fun, the child will be more likely to take a bath willingly.

Often kids refuse to take a bath because they're scared. The best way to deal with fear in little ones is to show true concern for their feelings. Use your imagination or tell them a story to help the fear go away. For example, put just a small amount of water in the tub with a few toys. Pretend it is an ocean and the child is a sailor or a mermaid. Tell her that her job is to rescue the boat or take care of a baby seal. Once she is okay with a small amount of water, add a little more (making sure the water you run into the tub is not hot).

Potty Training

Children at this age may be going through potty training. Learning to use the potty is a big step for a child. If you know the toddler is learning how to use the potty, have her sit on it several times throughout the day for a few minutes each time, especially right before bath time. This is good practice and often kids don't realize they have to go until they sit down. Also, remind her to try to go after eating and before going to bed.

Make sure the child flushes and washes her hands after she goes. Show her how happy and proud you are! This encourages her to continue trying the new potty routine until she has it down effortlessly.

Preschool-Aged Kids

A preschool bath kit should include fresh pajamas, fresh underwear, special age-appropriate soap and shampoo if provided, a cup for hair washing, a towel, and any requested games or toys.

By age three or four, kids generally have their bath routine down. They should be able to clean themselves, although you may have to help with the hair washing. You may not have to interact directly with them throughout the whole bath, as they may want to play with their bath toys or play make-believe alone, but *do not leave* the bathroom while the child is in the water.

School-Aged Kids

These kids are usually old enough to take a bath or shower by themselves and want their privacy, but go over the bathroom rules with the parents.

CHAPTER 10
Bedtime

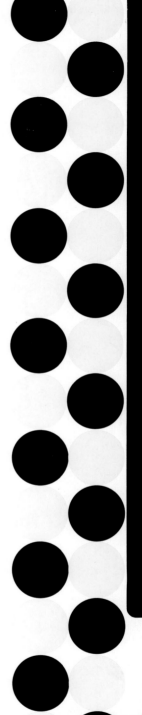

Night-Night!

If you're working a nighttime job, you will probably have to put the children you're watching to bed. Here are some tips you might find helpful.

Putting a Baby to Sleep

A baby is too young to know it's time to go to sleep and will often oppose you. Babies have tremendously different sleep patterns than older children because they have not yet determined their sleep/wake cycles. They'll sleep if they're tired. Many parents allow babies to follow their own schedule, which means that they eat when they're hungry and sleep when they're tired. It's especially important in this situation to be able to read a baby's cues. Babies sleep often because they get tired often. When they're tired but still awake, they get cranky. Cranky babies aren't a lot of fun. It's tough on the sitter to deal with a cranky baby and it's tough on the baby himself. Look for clues that the child is tired and try to get him down for a nap *before* he gets too cranky. This will also help prevent the baby from getting overtired. An overtired baby is even harder to get to sleep!

Some cues that a baby is tired include:

- He rubs his eyes
- He stares off into space
- He nods off
- He cries for no apparent reason
- He nuzzles into your chest
- He yawns

A baby generally sleeps better after having a bottle. If you see the baby getting sleepy, prepare a bottle and offer it to him before putting him down for his nap or for the night. Lullabies also help to calm and relax a child into a peaceful rest. If the parents have some lullaby or classical music CDs for the baby, these are good to play at nap- or bedtime. If you know you're watching a baby, you may want to bring some soothing music with you. If you don't have such a CD available, you can always sing to the baby.

When you put the baby into his crib, make sure that he is lying on his back. This is very important, as it allows the baby to breathe freely. Make sure not to put loose blankets, fluffy animals, or soft toys in bed with the baby, as this can also restrict breathing. If the child has a bumper on the crib, be sure it is tied on tightly. A crib bumper is the piece of padded fabric that you may see around the inside of the crib bars, usually tied on with five or six small strings across the bars. Bumpers are designed so the baby doesn't hit into the hard wood or plastic of the crib when sleeping, but they can be dangerous. If the baby pulls the bumper off, he can get twisted in it and choke or suffocate. That is why it is important to make sure bumpers are tied on tightly.

If you've put the baby down for a nap, it's a good idea to keep the lights on and stay actively noisy. Don't be too noisy, but make general household sounds, like watching TV or talking on the phone. If the baby has gone to sleep for the evening, keep the lights off in his room and try to be very quiet. This difference in environment helps the baby distinguish between bedtime and naptime. Regardless of whether he's napping or sleeping through the night, be sure to check on the baby frequently to make sure he is still lying on his back.

Remember, if the parents give you other instructions or have specific preferences, always put their requests first. Ask if you should wake the baby up after a certain length of time for a nap. Babies generally sleep for about 16 hours a day—usually distributed through a series of naps—and the parents may have a preferred sleep schedule for these naps.

How To Put a Toddler to Bed

A toddler is old enough to know about naptime or bedtime, and might also resist. Sleeping means an end to play, so resisting is natural. You can remind him that as soon as he wakes up it will be a new day filled with toys, games, and fun. You can also tell him that he can play anything he wants in his dreams once he's fallen asleep.

Ask the parents about the child's nighttime routine and rituals, such as picking out his pajamas, brushing his teeth, saying his prayers, or setting a cup of water on the nightstand. Find out if there is a special object, such as a blanket, a stuffed animal, or a doll that the child sleeps with. Holding onto this will help him fall asleep. It's also good to have the child hold the special nighttime object in the "getting ready for bed" time, right before he actually goes to sleep. These habits help a child get ready for bed subconsciously, and make an easy transition from the parents to you, the sitter. By repeating what the parents do, you will help the child recognize a pattern. It will make him comfortable knowing that you and his parents have the same routine. If it's okay with the parents, you can sing or read bedtime stories to help the child's transition to sleep.

Sometimes it helps to pat a toddler's back until he falls asleep. The human contact is important because it helps the child understand that he is not alone and is not being abandoned while you get to stay up late and have fun. If the child is still having trouble going to sleep, you may want to try lying down next to him and pretending to fall asleep. The child may be more okay with his own bedtime if he thinks it's your bedtime as well.

If the child still refuses to go to sleep, allow him to read or do a quiet activity in bed for a little while, as long as this is okay with the parents. This is also a good way for him to wind down and relax. Many children need to settle down and have some quiet, peaceful time before they actually fall asleep. It is best to discuss bedtime options with the parents and see what they recommend.

School-Aged Kids

An older kid is more independent when going to sleep. Let him follow his own routine of changing and washing up. Remind him about an hour before bedtime that it's almost time to turn in for the night, and do quiet activities during that time. Try to avoid running around before bedtime. Once he's dressed and ready for bed, ask him if he wants you to read to him. Older kids like chapter books. Try to find a calming story, not a violent, action-filled one.

If the child is having problems falling asleep, try a relaxation exercise. Tell him to close his eyes and imagine his head relaxing and going to sleep. Continue down to his toes, going from shoulders to arms to tummy to legs to feet.

Remember, your job doesn't end when the kids are asleep. Even if a child has gone to bed, he may still need you. A child may wake up because he had a bad dream or wants a drink of water. Kids also get up to go to the bathroom and may need your help. Don't get wrapped up in music, video games, or anything else that may distract you from a child's call from his bedroom, and check on him every half hour to make sure he is still okay.

How to Deal with Nightmares

If a little one wakes up crying, it is most likely from a nightmare or bad dream. Encourage the child to talk about his dream. Sometimes talking about the dream out loud will be enough to make the child feel better. If that doesn't work, try to figure out what you can do to help. For example, if the child dreamed that there was a monster under his bed, get a flashlight and look under the bed with the child to make sure there is no monster hiding there.

To help a child avoid having nightmares, it is best not to watch TV right before bedtime, especially anything with action, violence, or horror. If the child does have a nightmare, tell the parents when they get home.

CHAPTER 11

Babysitting for Children with Special Needs

Extra Care

You may be asked sometime in your babysitting career to watch a child with special needs such as a hearing problem, autism, or learning disability. You need to think about whether you would be comfortable in this situation. Remember, kids are kids, no matter the color, age, disability, or gender, but they are also very unique. When a child has a special need, it takes a little extra knowledge, patience, understanding, and acceptance from you as the babysitter.

All children are special. Children with disabilities are just as special, individual, and extraordinary as all other kids, they just have a special need that takes more focus and responsibility. Some people may call them "challenged" or "differently-abled." Try not to say "disabled" or "handicapped," which may be insulting or offensive to the child. Use the words that the parents use for the child's special need.

Before you accept a job, see if you can visit with the child while the parents are around to feel out the situation. This will not only give you a chance to get to know the child, it will help her feel comfortable with you, so that she won't feel as if she's been left with a stranger when her parents go away. Be honest with the parents as to how you feel about watching the child. If you aren't comfortable with the situation, you need to tell them. Taking on a job you don't think you can handle isn't good for anyone involved.

If you **do** decide that you would like to take on the challenge and feel comfortable with the situation, the first step is to discuss the child's **specific needs and disability** with the parents.

Communication

Communication is key to having a safe and happy time together. Learn the best way to communicate with the child. Ask how much she is able to understand, process, and remember. Some kids respond to direct eye contact whereas others may be turned off by this. Should you raise your voice, lower your voice, or talk at a steady pace? The child's parents can help fill in how best to communicate through the disability. Remember not to insult the child when communicating. Don't use baby talk just because you know she has a disability. Once you understand her level of understanding, it will be easier to communicate at that level, and not above or below it. Take her disability into consideration, but don't forget that she is still a kid, eager to learn, play, and be an individual.

Here are some important questions to ask the parents:

- Does the child have unique or different ways of communicating, such as special words, sounds, signs, or signals? If so, what are these?
- Does the child have difficulty interacting with others? This is especially important if she will be playing with other children.
- Can the child express her needs to you, such as being hungry or having to go to the bathroom?

Behavior

Learning about the child's behavior patterns will prevent surprises and increase positive interactions between you. Children with disabilities are often disciplined in different ways than the ones you may be familiar with. For example, a child with autism may not be able to sit in a "time out" chair after she hits her sister because she can't understand this punishment and it's not effective. A disabled child may process her own behavior differently and see the world differently than a nondisabled child, so be sure to ask the parents the best way to deal with negative behavior.

Some of the things you'll want to find out about the child's behavior:

- What might she do if she gets angry?
- How does she act when she's tired?
- Are there any special actions or behaviors you might see and how should you handle them?
- Does the child have any particular fears?

Ask the parents anything you can think of. As with all children, the more information you can gather the more enjoyable your time together will be.

Playtime

Disabled kids are still able to play, just in different ways. They may be into a different kind of toy or game, or have special tools they need to use.

Find out what the child's likes and dislikes are so you can design games around what she likes. For example, if she really loves knights and castles, you can play a make-believe story where she's a princess in a castle—ask about her kingdom and pet dragon. Or you may find out she loves coloring—you can rip up a paper bag, break out the crayons, and have an awesome coloring fest!

Some of the things you'll want to find out about the child's play habits:

- Does the child have any special play routines?
- Does she have any specific play-assistance equipment? If so, find out how it works.

- What toys and games does the child prefer?
- Is there anything specific that calms her down if she's upset?
- How closely does she need to be supervised, and how much help will she need? It may seem like the six-year-old you're watching can climb up the slide's ladder just fine, but her disability may interfere with her balance or confidence.

Ask parents tons of questions, and ask them to be specific with their answers. And above all else, be positive, be patient, and be respectful!

CHAPTER 12

Problems You May Encounter

Should I Babysit for a Sick Child?

Often parents need a babysitter when a child is sick because a daycare or pre-school won't take them. If you're out of school during a holiday or in the summer, you may be asked to watch a child who is ill.

First decide if that is a responsibility you want to take on. It is best to babysit after the first day or two of illness, after he sees the doctor. Remember, a sick child is cranky and needy when he's not feeling well, and he requires extra patience, sensitivity, and understanding. Also, he can be contagious. Before you babysit, ask the parents what illness the child has, whether he is contagious, if he has been to the doctor yet, and what extra care is needed.

Remember to be extra tolerant with a sick child—he will probably be grouchy, and could use some tender loving care.

What Happens if the Noncustodial Parent Comes Over Demanding to Take the Children?

What is the noncustodial parent? This is a parent that does not have legal custody of the child or children that you are babysitting. Custody means the right and responsibility to care for a child. Generally, divorced parents have joint custody, but if one parent does not have the legal authority to see his or her children, the parent who hired you should tell you. Ask them what procedure they want you to follow if the other parent shows up (such as calling a neighbor, their attorney, or the police). Taking a child away from the parent who has custody is a criminal offense.

If the parent comes to the house and you were told that he or she does not have custody, access, or visitation, do not let the parent inside. Most noncustodial parents do not have the keys for their ex's house. Call the custodial parent right away and ask how he or she wants you to proceed. If the noncustodial parent begins to harass or threaten you, call the police.

If the parent does have access to the house, do not physically try to stop the parent from taking the children. You and/or the children could be hurt in the process. Follow the instructions that the custodial parent gave you and call him or her right away.

If You Suspect Child Abuse

If you think a child is being abused, report it right away! Contact your local authorities or call a national child abuse hotline (such as, in the U.S., Childhelp, 1-800-4-A-CHILD). It's okay if you don't have any proof of abuse—it's not your job to prove it. You should be looking out for the best interests of the child. As long as you are honestly concerned, report suspected abuse or neglect immediately. You may save a child's life.

Write down as much information as you can about the child and family and the suspected abuse before you make the call. Include the names of the children and parents, their address, phone number, and how you know the family. Do you think the abuse is physical, emotional, sexual, or neglect? Write down examples of the suspected abuse, such as bruises, drawings of abuse, unnatural fears, or something the child told you. Make the phone call from your home and be prepared with a pen and paper to write down any information you are given. You may want to explain the situation to your parents and have them sit with you when you make the call. It is always helpful to involve an adult whom you trust.

Many cities or towns have their own abuse hotline or reporting number. Contact your local Child and Family Services, Child Protective Services, or Social

Services for assistance and further details. If you cannot find this number, call your local police and ask them for the number to report possible child abuse. Remember to stay calm and honest, and speak slowly and clearly on the phone. If you wish to remain anonymous, be sure you tell them.

Natural Disasters

What are natural disasters? These emergency situations are a form of extremely harsh weather, such as a tornado or hurricane. Extreme weather can be very destructive and scary, especially when you're babysitting. Learning how to prepare and how to deal with these disasters can help reduce the risk of both injuries and fear. Children may be especially frightened during such an overpowering event since their parents are not there. Remind the child that you'll be there for him and will look out for him until his parents are able to come home. If the child is scared of the storm, ease his fear with a story about the weather. Read some mythological tales about storms, like "Zeus and the Lightning," explain why

it rains from a scientific point of view, or tell a story about magical winds and miraculous thunderclaps. Whether the story is fiction or nonfiction, story time can help ease a child's fears and redirect his attention.

Be sure you call the child's parents during any threatening disaster. They may have an emergency plan for you to follow, such as going to a neighbor's house or having a friend pick you up. If you discussed a plan previously, be prepared to follow through with the instructions you were given.

Some natural disasters you may encounter are:

TORNADOES: If you see a tornado coming, or hear a tornado watch or warning on the radio or TV for your area, shut all doors and windows, and keep the radio or TV on to listen for updates. A "watch" tells you a tornado is possible and may be coming, while a "warning" tells you it *is* coming and you need to take action. When you hear there is a tornado warning, immediately go to the storm shelter, basement, or lowest part of the house with the children. If you can't find a room without windows, go to the center of a room as far away from the windows as possible, and sit on the floor with the kids. If there is a table nearby, pull it into the center of the room and sit under the table.

HURRICANES: If you hear a watch or warning on the radio or TV that a hurricane is in the area, shut all doors and windows, and keep the radio or TV on to listen for updates. If you're not told to evacuate, stay indoors! Get a flashlight and turn off any electrical devices you had been using, like the computer. Collect some play items that you can easily carry, like coloring books and crayons, storybooks, or a stuffed animal, and go to the storm shelter, basement, or lowest part of the house with the children. If you are in a room that has windows, go to the center of the room, as far away from the windows as possible, and sit on the floor with the kids. If you are told there is an evacuation of your area, dress yourself and the children in rain gear—long cotton shirts and pants, hats, raincoats, and rain boots. Don't take an umbrella because the high winds will tear it away. If you cannot reach the parents by phone, leave them a note or voicemail saying where you are going and with whom. Then head to the closest neighbor and follow him in the direction of evacuation.

FLOODS: If you hear a watch or warning on the radio or TV, shut all doors and windows, and keep the radio or TV on to listen for updates. If you are told there is an evacuation of your area, leave immediately. If you cannot reach the parents by phone, leave them a note or voicemail saying where you are going and with whom. Flooding happens very fast. Head to the closest neighbor and follow her in the direction of evacuation to higher ground. If you walk into water any deeper than your ankles turn around and go another way. Do not let the children try to play in the water. Standing water and deep water can be very dangerous.

VOLCANOES: If you hear about a nearby volcano eruption on TV or the radio, close all windows, air vents, or anything leading to the outdoors (such as a chimney flue) so the ash will not enter the house. If you are told there is an evacuation for your area, be sure to listen to the details of the evacuation plan. It is important to know in which direction to go. Dress yourself and the children in the most protective outfits you can find, such as cotton pants, long-sleeved shirts, and hats. Falling ash is made up of tiny little pieces of rock and glass, and can be very harmful to a person's lungs. Grab damp cloths to put over your noses and mouths to protect yourself and the kids from breathing in the ash. Help children younger than two years old hold the cloth. If you cannot reach the parents by phone, leave them a note or voicemail saying where you are going and with whom. Then head to the closest neighbor and follow him in the direction of evacuation.

WILDFIRES: If you hear a watch or warning on the radio or TV that a wildfire is nearby the house you are babysitting in, shut all doors and windows and keep the radio or TV on to listen for updates. If you are told there is an evacuation of your area, dress yourself and the children in the most protective outfits you can find, such as cotton pants, long-sleeved shirts, hiking boots or study shoes with thick soles, and hats. If you cannot reach the parents by phone, leave them a note or voicemail saying where you are going and with whom. Then head to the closest neighbor and follow her in the direction of evacuation.

While waiting out the weather, you can play make-believe games, sing songs, or tell stories. If the child is old enough to understand what is going on, reassure her that you will do everything you can to protect her.

Remember that not all natural disasters occur in every part of the country. Become familiar with the type of extreme weather your area has and discuss emergency plans with the parents of the children you are watching.

Congratulations on finishing *The Babysitter's Guidebook*!

You have taken a fantastic step to gaining more knowledge about safety, creativity, and child development. Not only will this help you become a better babysitter, it will also help you grow as a person and become more mature, resourceful, and independent.

Remember that the information you've learned in this guide may not apply to every babysitting situation. It's important to talk to the parents about their children, their home, and what they expect from you. You have acquired some great skills, and every babysitting job you take on will make you a better babysitter!

Bring this book with you when you go to your sitting jobs. You can refer to it for crafts, recipes, and safety questions, and take notes about the kids you watch.

Now score those jobs, get those art projects ready, and go have fun with the kids!

Best of luck,
Jill

BIBLIOGRAPHY

Bowlby, J. *Attachment*. Attachment and Loss, vol. 1. New York: Basic Books, 1969.

Broderick, P. C., and Blewitt, P. *The Life Span: Human Development for Helping Professionals*. Upper Saddle River, NJ: Merrill/Prentice Hall, 2003.

Garner, P. & Power, T. "Preschoolers' Emotional Control in the Disappointment Paradigm and Its Relation to Temperament, Emotional Knowledge, and Family Expressiveness." *Child Development* 67(4) (1996): 1406–19.

Hetherington, E. M., and Parke, R. D. *Child Psychology: A Contemporary Viewpoint,* 5th ed. New York: McGraw-Hill, 2003.

INDEX

A

Activities and crafts
  about: drawing with
    children, 64; make-
    believe guns, 60;
    overview and
    planning, 59–60
  arts and crafts, 61–70
  disabled kids and,
    95–96
  for elementary
    schoolers, 37–40
  for infants, 29, 30–31
  for kids of all ages,
    60–70
  for preschoolers, 35–36
  for toddlers, 32–34
Advertising, 6–9
Age groups. *See*
  Elementary
  schoolers; Infants;
  Preschoolers;
  Toddlers
Answering door, 23, 25

B

Babysitting jobs. *See*
  also Information to
  know (before parents
  leave); Safety

arriving on time,
  17–18
comforting kids, 41–
  42, 45–52
getting home after, 26
interviewing for. *See*
  Interviews
leaving house, 25
making good
  impression, 17–18
parents late coming
  home, 24–26
payment for, 24. *See*
  also Hourly rates
what to wear, 17
Bathing kids, 25, 81–86
Bedtime, 25, 87–91
Business cards, 6–8
Business of babysitting.
  See also Hourly rates
  advertising, 6–9
  requirements for, 1
  resume for, 1–4

C

Child abuse, suspecting,
  98–99
Child information
  sheets, 19–20,
  115–117

Clothing, what to wear,
  11, 17
Comforting kids, 41–42,
  45–52
Co-op babysitting, 14
CPR/First aid, 5
Crying, 31, 42, 45–46,
  51, 91

D

Diapers, changing, 25,
  46, 47
Disabilities. *See* Special-
  needs children

E

Elementary schoolers
  (age 5-10)
  activities for, 37–40
  bathing, 86
  comforting, 52
  putting to bed, 90–91
  what to expect, 37,
    38–39
Emergency information,
  18, 119–123

F

Fighting, 53–58
Fire safety, 21, 102

ABOUT THE AUTHOR

JILL D. CHASSÉ has been working with children for over 15 years. In high school she was the president of the Babysitters Club of Cedar Grove, coordinating part-time childcare and summer play activities. After high school, she began teaching at child development centers and became director of her first center in 1998. Chassé ran the Club Mom program at a child play center in Bethesda and Germantown, Maryland, and taught the Department of Education's Balls and Ramps program in Montgomery County, MD.

After college she became a consultant to numerous child-development centers, assisting with curriculum development, teacher training, and licensure requirements. She achieved her certification for pregnancy counseling in 1997 and has worked closely with parents regarding perinatal mental health and child development issues for over ten years. Dr. Chassé went on to earn a master's degree in public administration and a master's degree in psychology, concentrating in developmental and family psychology. She recently completed her doctorate in health administration, focusing on maternal/perinatal mental health and wellness. Currently, Jill Chassé works in the DC area in health and safety program management and lives in Brookeville, Maryland, with her family.

ABOUT THE ILLUSTRATOR

JESSICA SECHERET was born in a small French town. She attended the famous *École Boulle* in Paris where she learned furniture design. After several years spent in various agencies of architecture, she decided to give up squares, rulers, and compasses and put her body, heart, and soul into what she always loved—putting her own imagination on paper. She's currently residing at her studio in Paris, drawing for magazines and children's books. Some of her clients include American Girl, Running Press, Girl Scouts of America, Harper Collins, and Klutz Press.

Date of Job: ....

Start Time: .... End Time: ....

Parents' Names: ....

Kids' Names: ....

Hourly Rate: ....

How will I get there/home?: ....

Date of Job: ....

Start Time: .... End Time: ....

Parents' Names: ....

Kids' Names: ....

Hourly Rate: ....

How will I get there/home?: ....

Date of Job: ....

Start Time: .... End Time: ....

Parents' Names: ....

Kids' Names: ....

Hourly Rate: ....

How will I get there/home?: ....

Date of Job:

Start Time: .... End Time:

Parents' Names:

Kids' Names:

Hourly Rate:

How will I get there/home?:

Date of Job:

Start Time: .... End Time:

Parents' Names:

Kids' Names:

Hourly Rate:

How will I get there/home?:

Date of Job:

Start Time: .... End Time:

Parents' Names:

Kids' Names:

Hourly Rate:

How will I get there/home?:

Date of Job: ....

Start Time: .... End Time: ....

Parents' Names: ....

Kids' Names: ....

Hourly Rate: ....

How will I get there/home?: ....

Date of Job: ....

Start Time: .... End Time: ....

Parents' Names: ....

Kids' Names: ....

Hourly Rate: ....

How will I get there/home?: ....

Date of Job: ....

Start Time: .... End Time: ....

Parents' Names: ....

Kids' Names: ....

Hourly Rate: ....

How will I get there/home?: ....

Date of Job: ....

Start Time: .... End Time: ....

Parents' Names: ....

Kids' Names: ....

Hourly Rate: ....

How will I get there/home?: ....

Date of Job: ....

Start Time: .... End Time: ....

Parents' Names: ....

Kids' Names: ....

Hourly Rate: ....

How will I get there/home?: ....

Date of Job: ....

Start Time: .... End Time: ....

Parents' Names: ....

Kids' Names: ....

Hourly Rate: ....

How will I get there/home?: ....

CHILD INFORMATION SHEET

Child's name: ....

Nicknames(s): ....

Date of birth: .... Age: ....

Allergies: ....

Medications: ....

Special instructions: ....

Naptime: .... Bedtime: ....

Meal times: (B) ...... (L) ...... (D) ......

Are snacks okay?: [Y] [N]

Favorite games and activities: ....

Favorite songs: ....

Favorite toys: ....

Friends: ....

Other notes: ....

CHILD INFORMATION SHEET

Child's name: ....

Nicknames(s): ....

Date of birth: .... Age: ....

Allergies: ....

Medications: ....

Special instructions: ....

Naptime: .... Bedtime: ....

Meal times: (B) ...... (L) ...... (D) ......

Are snacks okay?: [Y] [N]

Favorite games and activities: ....

Favorite songs: ....

Favorite toys: ....

Friends: ....

Other notes: ....

CHILD INFORMATION SHEET

Child's name: ....

Nicknames(s): ....

Date of birth: .... Age: ....

Allergies: ....

Medications: ....

Special instructions: ....

Naptime: .... Bedtime: ....

Meal times: (B) ...... (L) ...... (D) ......

Are snacks okay?: [Y] [N]

Favorite games and activities: ....

Favorite songs: ....

Favorite toys: ....

Friends: ....

Other notes: ....

CHILD INFORMATION SHEET

Child's name: ....

Nicknames(s): ....

Date of birth: .... Age: ....

Allergies: ....

Medications: ....

Special instructions: ....

Naptime: .... Bedtime: ....

Meal times: (B) ...... (L) ...... (D) ......

Are snacks okay?: [Y] [N]

Favorite games and activities: ....

Favorite songs: ....

Favorite toys: ....

Friends: ....

Other notes: ....

CHILD INFORMATION SHEET

Child's name: ....

Nicknames(s): ....

Date of birth: .... Age: ....

Allergies: ....

Medications: ....

Special instructions: ....

Naptime: .... Bedtime: ....

Meal times: (B) .... (L) .... (D) ....

Are snacks okay?: [Y] [N] ....

Favorite games and activities: ....

Favorite songs: ....

Favorite toys: ....

Friends: ....

Other notes: ....

CHILD INFORMATION SHEET

Child's name: ....

Nicknames(s): ....

Date of birth: .... Age: ....

Allergies: ....

Medications: ....

Special instructions: ....

Naptime: .... Bedtime: ....

Meal times: (B) .... (L) .... (D) ....

Are snacks okay?: [Y] [N] ....

Favorite games and activities: ....

Favorite songs: ....

Favorite toys: ....

Friends: ....

Other notes: ....

CHILD INFORMATION SHEET

Child's name: ....

Nicknames(s): ....

Date of birth: .... Age: ....

Allergies: ....

Medications: ....

Special instructions: ....

Naptime: .... Bedtime: ....

Meal times: (B) .... (L) .... (D) ....

Are snacks okay?: [Y] [N] ....

Favorite games and activities: ....

Favorite songs: ....

Favorite toys: ....

Friends: ....

Other notes: ....

CHILD INFORMATION SHEET

Child's name: ....

Nicknames(s): ....

Date of birth: .... Age: ....

Allergies: ....

Medications: ....

Special instructions: ....

Naptime: .... Bedtime: ....

Meal times: (B) .... (L) .... (D) ....

Are snacks okay?: [Y] [N] ....

Favorite games and activities: ....

Favorite songs: ....

Favorite toys: ....

Friends: ....

Other notes: ....

EMERGENCY INFORMATION SHEET

Family's name: ....

Child's name(s): ....

....

Address: ....

Nearest cross street: ....

Parents' phone number: ....

Emergency contact phone number
  (a close relative or neighbor): ....

....

Police / fire department: ....

Hospital: ....

Doctor's name and phone number: ....

....

Poison Control Center: ....

EMERGENCY INFORMATION SHEET

Family's name: ....

Child's name(s): ....

....

Address: ....

Nearest cross street: ....

Parents' phone number: ....

Emergency contact phone number
  (a close relative or neighbor): ....

....

Police / fire department: ....

Hospital: ....

Doctor's name and phone number: ....

....

Poison Control Center: ....

EMERGENCY INFORMATION SHEET

Family's name: ....

Child's name(s): ....

....

Address: ....

Nearest cross street: ....

Parents' phone number: ....

Emergency contact phone number
  (a close relative or neighbor): ....

....

Police / fire department: ....

Hospital: ....

Doctor's name and phone number: ....

....

Poison Control Center: ....

EMERGENCY INFORMATION SHEET

Family's name: ....

Child's name(s): ....

....

Address: ....

Nearest cross street: ....

Parents' phone number: ....

Emergency contact phone number
  (a close relative or neighbor): ....

....

Police / fire department: ....

Hospital: ....

Doctor's name and phone number: ....

....

Poison Control Center: ....